Brunner, Misunderstanding
the Church

260 B 89m

Resn

Küng 262.7 K96

Flew 225. 826 F61

232
R658   Robinson 233 R66
            "   261. R662

William 230.090
                        H 81
Hand 260 H 236

Jesus' Spiritual Journey

—and Ours

JESUS' SPIRITUAL JOURNEY —AND OURS

Thomas S. Kepler

PH.D., S.T.D., D.D.

Professor of New Testament

GRADUATE SCHOOL OF THEOLOGY
OBERLIN COLLEGE

THE WORLD PUBLISHING COMPANY

CLEVELAND AND NEW YORK

Published by The World Publishing Company

Library of Congress Catalog Card Number: 52–5185

3 W P455

Copyright 1952 by The World Publishing Company

TO

Florence, Ann, and Tom,
who in many ways have
helped me on my own
spiritual journey

CONTENTS

7

PREFACE

Two events are especially significant in the contemporary world of Christian thought: (1) The interest in the ecumenical movement, in which churches of all denominations are searching for the theological ideas and the ethical values which they share in common. The Assembly of the World Council of Churches at Amsterdam in the summer of 1948 was a high symbol of this attempt to knit the churches together in the spirit of universalism. (2) The concern for devotional literature. In recent years there has been a resurgence of publishing the devotional classics of the centuries and of writing fresh devotional literature by modern interpreters.

It seems obvious that these two factors of contemporary interest should go together, for the basic spirit of the ecumenical movement is to be found in the common prayer life of its members. Men may search for different authorities for their theological and ethical dogmas; but when they pray and worship, they speak a common spiritual language.

While interest has focused afresh upon the classical writings of the Christian centuries, the one book at the center of the devotional life is the Bible, and especially the gospels where the person of Jesus radiates in clear perspective. The Bible is still the "best seller" of all books. Modern man finds particularly in the Psalms, the writings of the Hebrew prophets, and the books of the New Testament an interpretation of life which fulfills his contemporary spiritual needs.

9

Centuries have not dimmed the devotional value of the religious views contained in these classical writings. The person of Jesus in particular speaks to modern man a word which seems "the hope of the world."

A modern writer views Jesus' contemporary value in clear words:

> *Jesus leaps in a unique way across the changing centuries because he spoke to the unchanging needs of the heart of man. Jesus speaks to us, not as an antiquated first-century theologian, but as one who knew what was in the heart of man. (He expounded no doctrines) but lived great life convictions, and hence speaks to the living experience of all time.*[1]

The forty studies in this book about Jesus were initially written for a newspaper-reading audience, being circulated as a column in metropolitan newspapers for forty consecutive days. The writer has tried to do several things in these pages: (1) to show Jesus in his native setting and the real life-problems which he faced; (2) to capture from Jesus' life and teachings some of the religious insights which possess (high contemporary value;) (3) to employ constructive results of scholarship in a study of the gospels; (4) to write the chapters in an idiom which the general audience can appreciate. The studies are based mainly on the chronology of events found in the Gospel of Mark, with supplementary materials from the Gospel of Matthew and the Gospel of Luke.

The author naturally hopes that these studies will help modern men and women understand and live the vital prin-

---

[1] Clarence T. Craig, *Jesus in Our Teaching* (New York: Abingdon Press, 1931), p. 116.

ciples of the Christian faith in the present world. It is his conviction that the ideas of the Hebrew prophets and the insights of Jesus compose a "design for living," which can save this world toward becoming the Kingdom of God on earth. In sharing "Jesus' spiritual journey—and ours," may the readers find a dynamic value in his spiritual companionship.

THOMAS S. KEPLER

Graduate School of Theology
Oberlin College
Oberlin, Ohio

Jesus' Spiritual Journey
—and Ours

THREE MODERN WISE MEN BOW
BEFORE JESUS

POETRY AND fact are beautifully entwined about the birth of Jesus. The diverse details in the gospels of Matthew and Luke glorify the birth of a Saviour. Luke (1:26–2:20; 3:23–38) depicts the manifestation of the Holy Spirit upon Mary and Simeon; angels mediate between God and the shepherds; Anna praises the one who would redeem Jerusalem; this Divine Messenger, whose genealogy is traced to Adam, born amidst angelic praises and God's hovering care, is the Saviour of the whole world!

Matthew (1:1–25) primarily concerns himself with Jesus as the Saviour of the Jews; he traces Jesus' genealogy only as far as Abraham, the great Jewish patriarch. Yet the Magi of the East, in conferring gifts of gold, frankincense, and myrrh at Jesus' birthplace, show that he is also a Saviour at whose feet the Gentiles bow. The forces of nature, by having the star in the east guide the wise men, add wonder to this Saviour's birth.

Prophecy is fulfilled at Jesus' birth: He is born of a virgin, in keeping with Isaiah; his birthplace is Bethlehem, as announced by Micah; Herod issues a decree to slay male babes under two years of age, fulfilling Jeremiah's prophecy. The forces of nature, the wise men of the Gentile world, and the hopes of Israel unite in this awesome moment in history to pay reverence to a Saviour.

Wise men bowed before Jesus in the year 4 B.C., guided to his birthplace by the star in the east. Wise men today continue to revere Jesus. As modern seers look into the mysterious universe, as did the wise men of old, and discern the nearest light star, Alpha Centauri, twenty-five billion miles away, their need of a "saviour" is as deep as that of the wise men of old guided by their star in the east.

Three modern wise men tell us their thoughts as they pay reverence to Jesus. *The first of these wise men is the theologian.* This is his interpretation:

> *The Old Testament looked forward to the "day of the Lord" when God's Golden Age would find its setting in history. But it remained a future hope. When Jesus came, however, a "mystery" happened. History became the setting for divine things. Those who followed Jesus found a new lease on life. . . . Yes, Jesus owes His heritage to the prophetic tradition of Israel; and His spirit has been carried through the Christian centuries, though in a distorted way, by the church and its members. Yet Jesus is not to be classified with Socrates, Moses, Shakespeare, Dante, or Browning. We would arise to pay homage to these men: before Jesus we would kneel! Jesus is different in a mysterious way from any other historical character. Even the calendars were changed because of his*

16

birth. History could never be the same because Jesus lived.

The second wise man to pay reverence to Jesus is America's Pulitzer-prize-winner dramatist, Eugene O'Neill, in *Days Without End*. Here is his story:

John Loving, a Roman Catholic lad, prayed that his parents might not die. But their lives were not saved by a miracle; so John Loving lost his faith. He became outwardly a skeptic and a cynic, though inwardly he searched deeply for a way of life. He tried Oriental religions and philosophical cults; he joined an atheists' club. A friend, Father Beaird, stood by John Loving. When John said, "A new saviour must be born who will reveal to us how we can be saved from ourselves, so that we can be free of the past and inherit the future and not perish by it," Father Beaird replied, "You are forgetting that men have such a saviour, Jack. All they need is to remember him." . . . But John Loving was not to "remember him" until time had tired his search. The setting was a small chapel, silhouetted against the sky at dawn. Partly against his will, John Loving reluctantly walked into this chapel. Before a cross, dimly distinguished by the morning light coming through colored windows, John Loving knelt. For the first time since his parents' death he found peace. His prayer was: "Thou hast conquered, Lord. Thou art— the end. Forgive this damned soul of John Loving."

The third of our wise men is John Oxenham, the poet,
who passed away in 1941, the year the whole world was
at war. It was he who envisioned, in "No East or West,"
the way to universal peace, as he paid reverence to Jesus:

> *In Christ there is no East or West,*
> *In Him no South or North,*
> *But one great fellowship of Love*
> *Throughout the whole wide earth.*
>
> *In Him shall true hearts everywhere*
> *Their high communion find.*
> *His service is the golden cord*
> *Close-binding all mankind.*
>
> *Join hands then, Brothers of the Faith,*
> *Whate'er your race may be!*
> *Who serves my Father as a son*
> *Is surely kin to me.*
>
> *In Christ now meet both East and West,*
> *In Him meets South and North,*
> *All Christly souls are one in Him,*
> *Throughout the whole wide earth.*[1]

Seeing Christ through the eyes of these modern wise
men makes one feel anew:

[1] From *Bees in Amber* by John Oxenham. Reprinted by permission of
the American Tract Society.

Not the Christ in the manger;
Not the Christ on the cross.
But the Christ in the soul
Can save that soul,
When all but love is lost.

But such an experience begins with paying reverence to one born into the world as a Saviour! We begin "Jesus' spiritual journey—and ours" by meditating upon the mystery of his birth.

❧ 2 ❧

GOD BE IN ALL OF ME

FOR TWELVE years I taught religion in Lawrence College. Commencement exercises in that beautiful Wisconsin setting were always significant—there was usually a good speaker, an atmosphere of dignity, degrees were given to a fine group of young men and women. But the high moment of each commencement came as the benediction was sung by sixty voices in an *a cappella* choir:

God be in my head,
And in my understanding;
God be in my eyes,
And in my looking;
God be in my mouth,
And in my speaking;

God be in my heart,
And in my thinking;
God be at my end,
And at my departing.

The words, out of the *Sarum Primer* (1558), always seemed to have as much spiritual significance for twentieth-century college graduates as for the pre-Reformation liturgy of the Roman Catholic Church in England, Ireland, and Scotland (where the Sarum rites were originally used). Jesus, too, at his baptism became aware in an unusual way that God was in his understanding, his looking, his speaking, his thinking.

The baptism of Jesus is couched in poetic language and symbolism. It is a dramatic moment in Jesus' life when his daily work is shifted from the carpenter shop to preaching to men of God's Kingdom. Jesus at his baptism (Mk. 1:1–11) wished to unite himself with others to start the nation on a new beginning, so that God might give His Kingdom to His people: he felt himself uniquely called to prepare mankind for God's coming Kingdom. Words of consecration and symbols are associated with his baptism: "Thou art my beloved Son" is the coronation statement to be heard by a Messianic king (Psalm 2:7); "With thee I am well pleased" is the consecration statement given to the Servant of the Lord (Isa. 42:1); the descent of the dove symbolizes the life-giving Spirit of God (which hovered over the creation), the spirit of wisdom (as taught by the rabbis), the spirit of gentleness. The gospel portrait thus sees Jesus as the recipient of

God's power, wisdom, and love. That John baptized Jesus with water is part of the factual narration: that Jesus was baptized with God's Spirit is central to the gospel story. The event as a whole represents what the early Christians thought about Jesus: He is God's beloved Son in whom God is well pleased.

In a relative way, Jesus' baptismal experience is shared by his followers today, as they see their missions under the focus of God. Listen to Fred Stone, the actor, tell of his "spiritual baptism" to a group in Billings, Montana:

> I had a feeling that I was still an outsider—you know—that I was still outside of the Kingdom of God. I hadn't done anything yet. I didn't feel as if I were in! I wanted to be inside looking out. I wanted to make a stand once and forever before that meeting closed. I told them of my life, of how I had been on the stage since I was nine—which meant forty years. I told them that I had made a fortune; of my wife and children; of how I had climbed the ladder of success, but that I hadn't taken even a single step on the golden ladder of spiritual things, and that I was going to start that very day. Then I said the Lord's Prayer and the meeting ended.

Jesus has been described as a "once-born" man, while the rest of us are "twice-born" persons. His baptismal experience was an extraordinary experience of God, in which he saw deeply his mission in laboring for God's Kingdom. Our spiritual baptisms too are unique experiences for us when we see ourselves with our talents fully dedicated as instruments to bring God's Kingdom into the world. Saul Kane, in Masefield's "Everlasting Mercy," sensed the meaning of spiritual baptism,

> *I knew that I was done with sin;*
> *I knew that Christ had given me birth*
> *To brother all the souls on earth.*[1]

A quarter of a century ago I heard Dr. George A. Gordon preach many Sundays in Old South Church, Boston. No man more resembled a great spiritual seer. His prayers always carried one up the altar stairs to God. He too had his spiritual baptism:

> *I recall an experience in Appleton Chapel; it came in a flash; it came to stay; it has been a permanent light. Weary with work, tired in nerve, waiting for the service to begin, I asked myself this question: What is it all for, this toil and struggle, living in the heart of intellectual conflict, nothing sure, what is the good of it? Then came this thought: Life stands at the center of the world, human life; whatever cleanses that, whatever redeems it from the power of evil, whatever gives it freedom, whatever greatens it and glorifies it, must be true. . . .*

God be in my understanding—in my looking—my speaking—my thinking—my departing. God be in all of me—is at the heart of "everyman's" baptism.

[1] From *Poems* by John Masefield. Copyright 1935 by the author. Reprinted by permission of The Macmillan Company, publishers.

TIME TO SPARE FOR GOD

WHILE A student in Cambridge University over twenty years ago, I read *Old Pybus* by Warwick Deeping. Because the story was set in Cambridge, England, its characters seemed to live for me. Its main character, Old Pybus, a caretaker at one of the colleges, and grandfather of a Cambridge student (to whom his identity was unknown), portrays depth, poise, dignity, honesty, patience, courage. You deeply admire him. At one place in the novel, Pybus gives us the secret of his ability to live better than his circumstances, when he says, "I love to relax at times and allow the sources of the Divine to flow through my whole life." He took seriously the words written by the author of *The Imitation of Christ:* "Blessed is the man who has time to spare for God."

Today we are sharing a forty-day spiritual journey with Jesus (Mk. 1:12, 13), who "has time to spare for God." Before Jesus begins his public ministry he feels the necessity to be alone with God, in order that he may look within his own breast and communicate with God about his labors for God's Kingdom. Jewish thought believed that God tested the righteous, so that their faithfulness would overflow to the glory of God. Jesus' victory over temptation in this forty-day trial serves as a prologue to the gospel story where Jesus in his public ministry will defeat the forces of evil. In the Bible forty days is a symbolic number of "time to spare for God": Moses was on Mount Sinai for forty days; Elijah fasted for forty days at Mount Horeb; Noah spent forty days on the ark during the flood. Jesus, like his predecessors in Jewish history, will find God's will during the forty days of meditation.

"Lent" is the name we give in the Christian calendar to this forty-day spiritual pilgrimage. The term "Lenten" originally meant "spring," the period when the days begin to "lengthen." In Christianity it became the forty-day period before Easter, beginning on Ash Wednesday and extending to the Saturday before Easter, excluding the Sundays of that period. It is a time of penitence in which Christians devote especial attention to the deepening of their spirituality.

We, like Jesus, need "time to spare for God." The Pythagoreans demanded that a young man spend a year in meditating upon the first principles of that movement before he could join as an initiate. A Christian likewise is obligated to take time from the active, busy events of life to think deeply upon the first principles of his faith: What is the purpose of my life? What does Jesus mean to me? What do I believe about God and immortality? Many of us feel the reality of Alfred Noyes' words:

> ... I am full-fed and yet
> I hunger!
> Who set this fiercer famine in my maw? ...
> Who set this deeper hunger in my heart?[1]

[1] From "Enceladus," Collected Poems of Alfred Noyes, vol. 1. Copyright 1909, 1913 by the author. Reprinted by permission of J. B. Lippincott Company, publishers.

And perhaps this "deeper hunger" is but the blessedness which Jesus expressed: "Blessed are those who hunger and thirst for righteousness, for they shall be filled." "Time to spare for God" can satisfy this spiritual gnawing.

A great mathematician said several years ago: "Religion is what one does with one's solitariness. A person will never be deeply religious, unless he takes time to practice solitude." Jesus used forty days in the wilderness "to practice solitude"; he continued to use solitude in his ministry on the Mount of Transfiguration, on the Mount of Olives, in the Garden of Gethsemane. Through solitude he found more deeply God's purpose for him—and so can we.

A person taken ill suddenly in a Canadian town was forced into solitude. He tells of his experience:

> *When I came to consciousness, I found myself in a small hospital room. The walls were white and clean. Dazed by the shock and weak with pain, my eyes wandered wistfully about the room. At last they fell upon a crucifix hanging alone on the white wall at the foot of my bed. The moment I gazed upon it a feeling of great peace came over me, and it seemed that I heard again the ancient words, "Lo, I am with you alway, even unto the end of the world."*

We of the Western world are accused of being over-active in religious living; we do not have enough "time to spare for God." Do we not need to dethrone speed and noise, and replace them with poise and silence? To think more seriously upon the meaning of Jesus Christ? During Lent, in a special way, we "take time to be holy." This forty-day period considers Jesus' spiritual journey— and ours. Let us remember the words of a Hindu proverb: "You only grow when you are alone"—and especially alone with God!

✦ 4 ✦

NOT BY BREAD ALONE

THE GOSPELS do not portray a narrative merely about *Jesus*; it is a story about Jesus *Christ*—"the beginning of the gospel of Jesus Christ, the Son of God" is the way the Gospel of Mark begins. Why Jesus is baptized by his cousin John is not altogether obvious in the gospels. The result of the experience, however, is clear: Jesus feels the Spirit of God call him, as never before, to his life mission. Yet to what type of mission? Is Jesus to become an economic reformer to satisfy material needs of the common people of Judaism (Mt. 4:1–4)? Certainly a person must be able to make a living before he can make a life—or is it just the opposite?

Steinbeck wrote *Grapes of Wrath* in 1939, depicting three hundred thousand "Okies," deprived of their land in Oklahoma, intent amid hardships on making their way to California where a living might be earned. Man

must work; and unless he can satisfy his material hunger, ,
there is little purpose in talking to him of spiritual satis-
faction. In 1929, eighty-five per cent of the people in the
United States did not have a decent standard of living.
During World War II, when wages were high, the Heller
Budget determined that an average family ought to have
at least $2,900 a year; yet figures showed that seventy per
cent of the families were receiving less than $2,000 a year.
The need of bread to satisfy physical hunger, and the
"bread of the spirit" to satisfy spiritual gnawing, is ever
with us.

Jesus lived amid devastating economic conditions. The
mass of the people in his day were peasants with small
land holdings which required long, hard work to make a
living. Often after one or two bad crops, a farmer would
lose his farm for lack of reserve wealth. A farm went by
inheritance to the oldest son. Where there was more than
one son, the others were often forced to beg or steal, or
become hirelings to wealthy land owners. Taxation was
an excessive burden: frontier taxes doubled the initial
price of a commodity; taxes were assessed on trees, cattle,
land, salt, marriage; a poll tax was paid on occupations;
taxes were paid to both Temple officials and the Roman
government. If Jesus were to initiate an economic reform
for his countrymen, the success of his ministry would not
long be in doubt.

Centuries earlier, during the Babylonian exile (597–
538 B.C.), a great poet envisioned the restoration of the
Jewish nation. For that new age the Lord promised:

27

On all roads they shall feed,
And on all bare heights shall be their pasture;
They shall not hunger nor thirst. (Isa. 49:10)

Perhaps Jesus is reflecting on these words in the temptation experience. If Jesus feels himself called by God to
bring His Kingdom into the world, must he not do away
with hungering and thirsting of the people? In his own
experience Jesus realizes that he has forsaken the material security of the carpenter shop to call men to perform
God's will. Has he done the right thing? Clearly there
comes to him the memory of Israel in the wilderness.
God caused hunger to be a means of bringing Israel
closer to him in spiritual fellowship. And so it will be
with Jesus' Kingdom program. Later he will teach his
disciples: "Seek ye first the Kingdom of God and all
things else will be added unto you." Also from the Torah
(Law) Jesus remembers God's word to his chosen people:

Man shall not live by bread alone,
But by every word that proceeds from the mouth of God.
(Deut. 8:3)

Evelyn Underhill defines the minister's first task as
that of making people aware of God in worship; it is not
to rid the community of its economic disturbances. Out
of this right relationship with God, the worshipers receive
the dynamic of divine wisdom, power, and love to live in
right economic relations with their neighbors. Jesus like
Evelyn Underhill is not blind to the physical needs of

the people in his time. Yet he knows that an economic reform in Judaism without the initial spiritual reform of its members will not have lasting results. Irving Babbit has said that every economic problem roots into a political problem, which roots into a philosophic problem, which roots into a religious problem. It was so in Jesus' day. The spiritual reformation of the individual and the nation is the point where an economic reform of a nation begins.

William L. Stidger in his poem catches the insights of Jesus:

> *Man does not live by bread alone,*
> *The ancient writings say:*
> *Re-echoed on a lofty hill*
> *By Christ one vibrant day.*
>
> *Man does not live by bread alone,*
> *He lives by truth and right,*
> *By beauty, brotherhood, and hope.*
> *By laughter, dream, and light.*
>
> *Man does not live by bread alone,*
> *Born of the earth and sod,*
> *But by each word and thought that leaps*
> *Hot from the heart of God!*[1]

[1] From "Man Does Not Live by Bread Alone!", *I Saw God Wash the World*, by William L. Stidger. Copyright 1934 by The Rodeheaver Company, Indiana. Reprinted by permission of the publishers.

❦ 5 ❦

THE QUEST FOR CERTAINTY

A FEW years ago in *Harper's* magazine appeared an article, "After Religion What?", by Frank S. Hopkins. He cited his grandfather, an Episcopalian minister, going about his large country parish with a quiet, courageous serenity, because he had no questions about religion: he possessed a religious certainty. The grandson, however, found himself unable to accept his grandfather's theology; instead he inherited mental frustration and intellectual uncertainty—hence he had no religion. So he asks, "After Religion What?" A proper answer to him would have been: "After religion, *religion!* But tied to a theology which savors of as much depth and height for your age as your grandfather's theology seemed to have for his time!" Frank S. Hopkins represents the present quest for certainty in religion; it was also a desire in Jesus' time. Jesus' temptation to jump from the pinnacle of the Temple is an insight into his desire to give the people of his day a "sign" to satisfy their quest for certainty.

A Jewish *Midrash* (teaching) current in Jesus' time said: "When King Messiah is revealed, he comes and stands upon the roof of the Holy Place; then will he announce to the Israelites and say: Ye poor, the time of your redemption is come." The gospel story infers that Jesus is meditating upon this teaching in reference to his

30

mission of announcing God's Kingdom (Mt. 4:5–7). Likewise he reflects upon Psalm 91 in reference to his role:

For he shall give his angels charge over thee,
To keep thee in all thy ways.
They shall bear thee up in their hands,
Lest thou dash thy foot against a stone.

Jesus' temptation is that of doing something spectacular—like jumping from the Temple pinnacle—to attract people to his Kingdom program. Such would invite God to set aside His laws to show who Jesus is. However, even though Jesus can quote Scripture to prove the possibility of this kind of leadership for God, he does not resort to this spectacular method. He will not *force* the will of God; rather he will trust and obey God's will, and show others how the Kingdom of God can come into their lives through the normal, orderly spiritual laws of the universe.

Jesus' temptation to give "signs" to those who have a quest for certainty is but a prologue to the rest of his ministry. Galileans, disciples, Pharisees and others continue to ask "signs" of him regarding God and His Kingdom; the same quest is current today. Men want to be certain of God. Professor George Burman Foster expressed this through Christian eyes: "Oh, if we could only believe that God is as good as Jesus!" Men also want to be certain of God's final revelation through Jesus Christ: "Are you he, or shall we look for another?" is a question men ask today as they asked also during Jesus' earthly ministry.

Three scholars set out to understand the elephant: One sat in his study, behind closed doors, smoking his pipe, and meditating upon the "nature and existence" of the elephant; another went to the Congressional Library and read all he could upon the elephant; the third flew to India, and there made a first-hand study of the elephant in its environment. In our quest as to Jesus' relation to God, we need to meditate upon who he is and to read books which interpret him; but no person will ever establish certainty about Jesus as Lord of life or Messiah until he sees whether Jesus' insights into life, out of their native environment, support his highest ideals and bring him companionship with God. John Baillie of Edinburgh found his "sign" of Jesus' lordship in the gospel narratives, as he lived Jesus' insights therein embodied:

> I say—in full remembrance of the many puzzles and perplexities which the study of the New Testament still continues to present to me—that the light of Christian truth, which has illumined for me the dark and difficult road of life, nowhere shines with so clear and pure a radiance as just in the Synoptic story.

The "sign" of certainty that Beethoven's Fifth Symphony is beautiful is to hear it; the "sign" of certainty that Jungfrau with its awesome heights will fill you with wonder is to sit before its majestic beauty; the "sign" of certainty as to whether Jesus is the one to bring God's Kingdom is to follow his religious insights. Jesus did not jump from the Temple pinnacle to force God to show his Messiahship; he invited men to trust and obey God. Because of his conquest in the temptation we sing with the poet about him:

> *Jesus, whose lot was with us cast,*
> *Who saw it out, from first to last:*
> *Patient and fearless, tender, true,*
> *Carpenter, vagabond, felon, Jew:*
> *Whose humorous eye took in each phase*
> *Of full, rich life this world displays,*
> *Yet evermore kept fast in view*
> *The far-off goal it leads us to. . . .*
>
> *Would I could win and keep and feel*
> *That heart of love, that spirit of steel.*

 6

THEY TOOK HIM TO A MOUNTAINTOP

They took Him to a mountaintop to see
Where earth's fair kingdoms flung their golden net
To snare the feet and trick the souls of men.
With slimy craft and cynic guile they said:

If He but sees the glory and the pride,
The pomps and pleasures of this tinsel world,
He will forget His splendid, futile dreams;
And so they took Him up and tempted Him. . . .[1]

THESE WORDS which Winfred E. Garrison sings in "Temptation" about Jesus can be said also of Alexander, Nebuchadnezzar, Caesar, Charlemagne, Napoleon, Hitler, Mussolini, Stalin, and legions of others who have craved world power. Within the breast of many a leader has been the urge to be a "superman" who might bring his own country into leadership or free it from domination of other nations. And Jesus is no exception—he yearns that his own people might be freed from Roman tyranny, and live like free men (Mt. 4:8–11). Jesus, however, did not succumb to "the pomps and pleasures of this tinsel world."

The day in which Jesus lived was a difficult one for the Jewish nation. After the death of Herod the Great in 4 B.C., Archelaus his son ruled with a cruel hand in Palestine. At one time his soldiers killed three thousand Jews who were giving their offerings in the Temple; Jerusalem's finest buildings were pillaged and burned; Judah the Galilean terrorized the country around Nazareth; the Temple treasury was looted; Varus crucified two thousand men; publicans forcefully extorted outrageous taxes from the Jews; Quirinius, in A.D. 6, deepened the anger of the Jewish people by taking a census for the purpose

[1] From "Temptation" by Winfred E. Garrison. Reprinted by permission of the author.

of Roman taxation records. Pontius Pilate, the successor of Archelaus, carried into Jerusalem standards with the "divine" image of the Roman emperor on them; he robbed the Temple and slaughtered many Jews. Herod Antipas, ruler of Galilee, whom Jesus called "the fox," put John the Baptist to death. Between 67 B.C. and A.D. 39, two hundred thousand of Israel's finest manhood had been murdered by the Roman government.

"At this time," says Rabbi Joseph Klausner, "none dared take part in political matters or adopt a definite attitude towards the fortunes of his miserable but beloved fatherland: he might not even utter his ideas aloud. Spies were everywhere and police held the population in subjection: all alike were downtrodden and overcome by fear." [2]

How similar the regimes of Hitler in Nazi Germany and Stalin in Communistic Russia are to the Roman rule of Jesus' era. How frequently history repeats itself—and how freshly Jesus' insights concerning world problems resound in each generation. Even Napoleon saw his own folly as compared to Jesus' wisdom:

> *Alexander, Caesar, Charlemagne and myself founded empires; but upon what did we rest the creations of our genius? Upon force. Jesus Christ alone founded His empire upon love, and at this hour millions of men would die for Him. . . . The religion of Christ is a mystery which subsists by its*

[2] From *Jesus of Nazareth* (New York: The Macmillan Co., 1929), p. 167.

*own force, and proceeds from a mind which is not
a human mind. Jesus exhibited in Himself the perfect example of His precepts. Jesus came into the
world to reveal the mysteries of heaven and the laws
of the Spirit.*

Strange words—yet wise words—to come from one of
the great world generals, who from his "mountaintop"
would rule the world with force!

Jesus looked back upon the history of his people: How
they had been persecuted continuously by the Egyptians,
the Syrians, the Medes and the Persians, the Assyrians,
the Greeks, the Babylonians, the Romans! He remembered how Judas Maccabeus, in 165 B.C., had with the
sword been victorious against Antiochus Epiphanes, after that tyrant had desecrated the Jerusalem Temple and
had slain many of the Jews; on December 25, 165 B.C.,
Judas Maccabeus with the Jewish "red-bloods" recap-
tured the Temple for Judaism. Yet Jesus also remembered that every conqueror of the Jews had finally gone
the way of defeat; those who had used the sword in world
conquest had perished with the sword. As we evaluate
Jesus' mountaintop meditation on the lure of political
power, these words convince us of the wisdom of his
decision:

*Speak, History! Who are Life's victors? Unroll
thy long annals and say: Are they those whom the
world called the victors, who won the success of a*

36

day? The martyrs, or Nero? The Spartans who fell
at Thermopylae's tryst, or the Persians and Xerxes?
His judges or Socrates, Pilate or Christ?[3]

Jesus leaves the temptation scene sure of his purpose:

From this moment onwards two courses were set
clearly before Jesus. He might adopt the views cur-
rent among his contemporaries and the methods of
force....On the other hand, he might follow the
path trodden by the ideal Servant of God depicted
in Isaiah 53, a path which led through suffering, mis-
understanding, and rejection to condemnation and
death. ... The one was the short and easy road, and,
with the miraculous powers which Jesus believed
himself to possess, would have succeeded—to out-
ward appearance. The other was the slow and diffi-
cult course, bringing on himself untold agony, and
promising for the immediate future only, a very
small measure of success.[4]

Reflecting upon the Torah (Law), Jesus concluded in
the wilderness:

You shall worship the Lord your God,
And him only shall you serve. ... And then ...

From the mountain peak He raised His eyes,
And saw the deep, calm sky, the stars, and God.

[3] William W. Story, "10 Victis."
[4] T. H. Robinson, *The Gospel of Matthew* (New York: Harper and
Bros., 1927), pp. 21, 22.

❦ 7 ❦

JESUS CAME PREACHING

D<small>R.</small> George A. Buttrick gave the Lyman Beecher Lectures on Preaching at the Divinity School of Yale University in 1930. He entitled his series, "Jesus Came Preaching." In these lectures he says:

> What was Jesus' authority? It was the authority of a Life! Truth is not a formula: it is a Life. Jesus was authority because in Him piercingly and persuasively Light broke upon our world[1]

Jesus as a preacher was not giving lectures to a classroom full of students; he was telling the Galilean crowds along the hillsides and the seashore: "The time is fulfilled, and the kingdom of God is at hand; repent, and believe in the gospel (Mk. 1:14, 15)." What Jesus preached was not something new; it merely re-echoed what prophets and preachers had been sounding for centuries—the coming of God's Kingdom! But in the one who "came preaching" people sensed an old message with a new authority, for

> One good man teaches many, men believe what
> they behold;
> One deed of kindness noticed is worth forty
> that are told...

[1] *Jesus Came Preaching* (Charles Scribner's Sons, 1931), p. 23.

*Though an able speaker charms me with his
eloquence, I say,*
I'd rather see a sermon than to hear one, any day.

The "good news" which Jesus announced about God's
coming Kingdom seemed to be incarnate in him. A later
interpreter of Jesus said, "He is the way, and the truth,
and the life." His preaching was so effective that old
words like "door," "yoke," "bread," "shepherd" took
upon new meaning because of the depth he gave to them:
"I am the *bread* of life. . . the *door*. . . the *good shepherd*.
. . . Take my *yoke* upon you." At the center of Jesus'
preaching was the Kingdom of God, which men were not
to build by keeping rules, but to receive out of God's
mercy and generosity.

A modern interpreter says that the first task of the
minister is to make his people, by his preaching, aware
of the infinite majesty of God: parish work, administra-
tion of church business come later. Certainly God's holi-
ness was at the center of Jesus' preaching. Paul the apostle speaks about "the foolishness of preaching"; and some
preaching is foolish, for it misses the point of meeting
real life-problems. T. S. Eliot, well-known literary critic,
once said, "If I were young again, I would preach." Jesus
would have welcomed Eliot's statement, for he felt that
preaching was the most important business in the world.
He gave his life to preaching, and was finally crucified
because he believed his message was the truth. Emerson
once said of a friend, "What you are speaks so loud that

39

I cannot hear what you say." So might it be said of Jesus. Some of Jesus' words were forgotten; but his life was remembered. John Knox has said that the early church was composed of those who remembered Jesus:

> The most important thing about the religious and ethical teachings of Jesus is not that he taught them but that he thought them. If Jesus had not taught in any formal way at all, or if, he having done so, his companions had completely forgotten his words, even so the church would still have come into being. For the church was created around a person, not a teaching; historically the greatest value attaching to Jesus' words is that they indicate so much as to his own character.[1]

Jesus came preaching—and through the Christian centuries preaching has been vital: Bishop Ambrose's preaching attracted Augustine to Christianity; John Wesley's preaching saved England from a revolution and brought Christianity home to the masses; Luther's preaching in the sixteenth century brought God's grace to human hearts; Phillips Brooks by his sermons remade lives in Boston in the nineteenth cenutry. (But preaching is not just confined to the pulpit) I once heard Kreisler play his violin in Chicago, and each person left the concert hall that afternoon holding his head and shoulders higher—for Kreisler had "preached" on his violin. I sat one day in the Dresden gallery and looked

[1] *The Man Christ Jesus* (New York: Harper and Bros., 1941), p. 55.

upon Raphael's "Sistine Madonna"—Raphael's "preaching" with his artist's brush made many a life more Christian. I once heard a returned medical missionary "preach" about the needs of China and temporarily inspire hundreds in an urban community. I once knew a political-science college teacher whose "preaching" inspired students in all vocations of life to labor for God's Kingdom. . . .

Whittier, in thinking upon the influence of one of his "preaching" friends, remarked:

> *The dear Lord's best interpreters*
> *Are humble human souls;*
> *The Gospel of a life like hers*
> *Is more than books or scrolls.*

Jesus came preaching—and so must we if we are to follow him. His words to his initial disciples echo down the centuries to us today: "Not every one who says to me, 'Lord, Lord,' shall enter the kingdom of heaven, but he who does the will of my Father who is in heaven." Each man must preach "the gospel according to me."

❧ 8 ❧

TWELVE MEN SHARED HIS DREAM

CHRISTIAN saints are not necessarily geniuses, but rather ordinary people with sensitive capacities who are willing to let God magnify their abilities. Certainly the twelve disciples whom Jesus chose as his helpers lacked the spark of genius. They were men from the lower middle class—four of them were fishermen, one collected taxes, another belonged to a revolutionary political party (called the Zealots) (Mk. 4:18–22; 2:14; 3:13–19). Their names are usually listed: Peter and Andrew, James and John; Matthew (Levi) and Thomas, Philip and Bartholomew (son of Tolmai); James (son of Alphaeus) and Thaddeus, Simon the Zealot (Canaanite) and Judas Iscariot. Judas Iscariot was the only citizen of Judea; the rest came from Galilee.

Peter, James, and John formed Jesus' inner circle of friends. Peter he nicknamed "the rock," since he was sometimes unpredictable; James and John (sons of Zebedee) he nicknamed "sons of thunder," because of their energetic personalities. Like Gideon with his small band of three hundred to fight a mighty enemy, Jesus begins with twelve ordinary men to initiate the greatest religious movement in history. God has an unusual way of employing small groups of ordinary people for His Kingdom cause!

Leonardo da Vinci once said that minority groups are often lonely figures in the center of culture. Perhaps Jesus and the twelve at times felt this "loneliness," yet they knew that the hope of God's Kingdom rests upon the shoulders of the loyal few. Israel had in the past looked to "the remnant" as the small nucleus who would usher in God's Kingdom. The rabbis of Jesus' time kept saying, "As long as there are thirty righteous men in any generation, there is always hope for God's Kingdom coming on the morrow." Says G. K. Chesterton in one of his essays:

> *Whenever our civilization wants a library to be cataloged, or a solar system discovered, or any trifles of that kind, it uses its specialists. But when it wishes anything done which is really serious, it collects twelve of the ordinary men standing around. The same thing was done, if I remember right, by the Founder of Christianity.*

The preparation of men for God's Kingdom in Jesus' time was "really serious." It still is; and God knows how to work through minorities. Some time ago Albert Einstein said that if five per cent of the people in the world would really work for world peace, we could have that dream realized. "Less than one per cent of humanity have caused most of the world's major troubles," said a recent editorial. Perhaps Jesus felt that way. As twelve men share his dream of God's coming Kingdom, Jesus envisions His "kingdom come on earth as it is in heaven."

Aided by twelve disciples, Jesus begins his ministry in Galilee, with its mixed population of Jew and Gentile, remote from the rule of the Temple and the Sanhedrin (the Supreme Court of Judaism) at Jerusalem. Galilee had always been open to liberal, prophetic religion; and its great highways of travel running in all directions made it a center where Jesus' message would be heard and circulated by travelers. It is an ideal loca-

43

tion in which Jesus is to begin his Kingdom plans with his disciples.

We are now living in the modern world. "Ideals are still the world's masters. . . . He whom a dream hath possessed knoweth no more of doubting." Yet God's Kingdom will never come into the world merely by preaching theories about "World Christianity." Rather it will arrive in so far as there are active minority groups in our communities—"groups of twelve"—working out in small *cell groups* the essentials of World Christianity.

Several summers ago I gave a series of lectures to a group of seventy students in Golden, Colorado. Among them was a Jewish refugee from Austria, a student in Mount Holyoke College; a Roman Catholic girl from South America, with a doctor's degree in social science; a Chinese student, taking graduate work at Yale University; a Negro Protestant girl, taking pre-medical work at Fiske University; an American Japanese Nisei; students from Wesleyan, Oberlin, Wellesley, and other American colleges. These students were living together during the summer months, regardless of race, creed, culture. Part of the time was spent in thinking and studying together; the rest was used in doing social betterment work in Colorado communities. They felt that in small groups, minorities might live the pattern by which the whole world should become God's Kingdom.

That is the way today—as well as among the twelve— God wants us to share his dream of a coming Kingdom on earth! God's future Kingdom depends upon consecrated minorities—"groups of twelve"—who will share his dream! Let it be said of us, as of Jesus:

> *He saw through every cloud a gleam—*
> *He had his dream. . . .*[1]

A dream of God's Kingdom coming on earth!

❦ 9 ❦

THE IMITATION OF CHRIST

GERARD GROOT was one of Holland's most effective preachers in the fourteenth century. He awakened deep spiritual interest in the Christian faith; but because he criticized some of the ineffective aspects of the Church, the Bishop of Utrecht revoked his license to preach. Hence, in 1384, he retired to his home at Deventer. In the last year before his death he organized a vital spiritual lay movement called "The Brethren of the Common Life," and wrote *The Imitation of Christ*. His writings are permeated with the spirit of Christ; the lure of his movement was for his disciples to "imitate Christ"; and the heart of his teachings was, "Conquer yourself where you are." Gerard Groot seemed to catch the spirit of Christ in a deeply unique fashion. Since Groot's time *The Imitation of Christ* has gone through six thousand editions.

Discipleship to Jesus' first followers meant "the imita-

[1] From *The Complete Poems* of Paul Laurence Dunbar. Reprinted by permission of Dodd, Mead & Company, publishers.

tion of Christ." To Levi sitting at the tax office, he said "Follow me (Mk. 2:14)." To his disciples he gave the invitation: "If any man would come after me, let him deny himself and take up his cross and follow me (Mk. 8:34)." To the young ruler Jesus said: "Sell all you have and distribute to the poor; come, follow me (Lk. 18:22)." To the young man who would first go home to bury his father, Jesus said: "Follow me, and leave the dead to bury their dead (Mt. 8:22)." Then, as now, John Hunter's tender words describe the meaning of "imitating Christ":

> *Dear Master, in Whose life I see*
> *All that I long and fail to be;*
> *Let Thy clear light forever shine*
> *To shame and guide this life of mine.*
>
> *Though what I dream and what I do*
> *In my poor days are always two,*
> *Help me, oppressed by things undone,*
> *O Thou, Whose dreams and deeds were one.*

In 1896, Charles M. Sheldon wrote *In His Steps*, a story about what following Jesus can do for a community. Since its publication it has sold over twenty million copies and has been translated into twenty-one languages. In this novel Dr. Sheldon says:

> *Each individual Christian, businessman, citizen, needs to follow in His steps along the path of personal sacrifice for Him. There is not a different path*

*today from that of Jesus' own times. It is the same
path. The call is for a new discipleship, a new following of Jesus, more like the early, simple, apos-
tolic Christianity when the disciples left all and
literally followed the Master. Nothing but a discipleship of this kind can face the destructive selfishness of the age, with any hope of overcoming it.*

While Dr. Sheldon wrote these words over fifty years
ago, they resound as basic for the way out of our present
world dilemma.

Men have tried to imitate Christ through the centuries. To them we owe great debts for what they have
done to our heritage. In the eleventh century, Bernard
of Clairvaux preached "the imitation of Christ"; five
hundred monasteries resulted from his efforts, revitaliz-
ing much of Christian life in France. In the thirteenth
century Francis of Assisi, "the troubador of God," im-
itated Christ by living a life of poverty and ministering
to the poor; he founded the Franciscan order, becoming
the most beloved saint of the Middle Ages. According
to Evelyn Underhill, Francis "walked, literally, in an
enchanted world, where every living thing was a theo-
phany, and all values were transvaluated by love."
George Fox stressed "the imitation of Christ" in seven-
teenth-century England and walked by the "inner light"
of One who was "the light of the world"; he was im-
prisoned for his religious views, but he founded the
Society of Friends in 1652. John Wesley in eighteenth-

47

century England emphasized "the imitation of Christ" through his disciplines in *Christian Perfection*; the Methodist society in 1739 resulted, with its conversion of thousands of common men of England.

Great leaders today continue to "imitate Christ": Frank Laubach on the Island of Mindanao, teaches the ignorant to read and write. Muriel Lester in London aids the underprivileged in Kingsley Hall. Toyohiko Kagawa in Japan ministers to the downtrodden in a defeated country. Albert Schweitzer relieves pain of the natives in the Lamberéné Forest in Africa. Multitudes of men and women bring relief to their communities. These stress "the imitation of Christ."

To his first disciples Jesus said: "You are my disciples if you love one another (Jn. 13:35)." Though we today may not be able to decide all our theological problems about Jesus, we can imitate his way of love. Perhaps we need today something of the enthusiasm of a heathen sojourning in Galilee in A.D. 32:

> *If Jesus Christ is a man—*
> *And only a man—I say*
> *That of all mankind I cleave to him,*
> *To him will I cleave alway.*
>
> *If Jesus Christ is a God—*
> *And the only God—I swear*
> *I will follow him through heaven and hell,*
> *The earth, the sea, the air!* [1]

[1] From "The Song of a Heathen" by Richard Watson Gilder. Reprinted by permission of Houghton Mifflin Company, publishers.

Those today who practice "the imitation of Christ" are the hope of the world!

❧ 10 ❧

WE MUST LOOSEN THE FETTERS
THAT BIND

"Dear love, we must loosen the fetters that bind,
We must seek, we must find."

So sings Angela Morgan in one of her poems. So emphasized Jesus in his ministry of healing. Miracles of healing in the gospels about Jesus are not interferences with nature, but "signs" or "tokens" of a new life of power inaugurated by the coming of Jesus. The great "sign" of God's power at work in the Old Testament is the crossing of the Red Sea: had the Israelites remained in Egypt, instead of crossing the Red Sea into Sinai, there never would have been a religion of Judaism. The great "sign" in the New Testament is the resurrection of Jesus Christ: without the resurrection, the movement begun by Jesus would have ended as a hazy dream in the memories of Jesus' disciples, defeated by his death. Miracles in the gospels are "signs" to show God's power working in the world.

Miracle stories play a large role in the Gospel of Mark. Of its 661 verses, 209 (over thirty-one per cent) deal

49

with miracle events. Most of the stories show how "the fetters that bind" personalities are loosened by the power of the gospel of Jesus Christ. Jesus sends word by the disciples of John the Baptist: "Go your way, and tell John what things you have seen and heard; the blind receive their sight, the lame walk, the lepers are cleansed, the deaf hear, the dead are raised up, and the poor have good tidings preached to them (Lk. 7:22)."

Miracle stories in the gospels play an important role in the work of Jesus, never, however, to prove Jesus as the son of God, or to accredit his heavenly origin. Miracle events are primarily illustrations of God's power working in the life of man. "They are," A. M. Hunter says, "tokens of the coming of God's reign in Jesus. They are the Kingdom of God in action—God's sovereign grace and forgiveness operative in Christ. 'If I by the finger of God cast out devils,' says Jesus, 'then is the kingdom of God come upon you.' The miracles are signs, after all, but only signs for those whose spiritual insight enables them to discern the sovereign saving activity of God in Jesus."[1]

We believe today in a law-abiding universe; we trust the laws of nature. Yet it is not logical for modern man to say with Matthew Arnold, "Miracles do not happen," for "we cannot boast of knowing the laws of nature well enough to be certain whether a particular occurrence contravenes them or not." As one critic says, "Miracles

[1] *The Work and Words of Jesus* (Westminster Press, 1950), pp. 55, 56.

are miraculous only to those who are already prepared
to recognize the operation of God in the commonest
events and actions." The miracles in the gospels are not
so much stories about the way God changes his laws to
meet human whims, but rather the way by which God's
empowering Spirit changes the lives of men and women.

Modern illustrations show how persons empowered
with "Christian faith" loose "the fetters that bind"
(called "the driving out of demons" in the gospel language). *The Seale-Hayne Neurological Journal,* with its
post-war cases of World War I, tells of the blind, the
deaf, the dumb, and the paralytic nursed back to nor-
malcy through the aid of kind, wise, considerate doctors,
ministers and nurses: A man blinded by shell shock
finally is able to return to his work as a watch repairman.
A German soldier, lying on his bed with paralyzed limbs,
stands on his feet and walks when awarded the Iron
Cross by his commanding officer. Dr. Paul Du Bois describes a patient who became paralytic in her limbs following a fit of anger, but who was healed in three days so
that she could walk again.

Such illustrations help us to see in part how Jesus'
insights placed his followers in such a relationship to
God that He, through His laws, is able to bring them
power and help today as well as in the first century.
Amid the tensions of the first century, caused by the
Roman government and the harsh demands of life in
Palestine, Jesus did not advise his followers to dodge the

issues of life. Rather he taught them to face their crises in such a way that they could utilize the spiritual energies which God would give to them. The great "miracle" of Jesus' own life—calm, trusting, courageous—was an invitation to his followers to believe that he was the messenger of a new age in history:

"Dear love, we must loosen the fetters that bind,
We must seek, we must find."

⊰⊱ 11 ⊰⊱

LET HIM STAND AS HAVING POWER

IN HIS parables Jesus frequently shows that the God who works in nature is active also in the life of man. The power of life working in the mustard seed, which causes a little speck to grow into a tree, is illustration of the dynamic of God's Spirit empowering the life of man. Were Jesus teaching today we can well imagine him saying: "Consider atomic energy, how the scientist can within a small metal case corral enough energy from the universe to blow up a modern city. This is not a 'dead' universe, but one filled with energy. As the scientist has learned how to tap the energy of the universe for his purpose, so I show you how to find access to God's power for your daily living."

Many of Jesus' "miracles" can be classified as *healings*: Peter's mother-in-law is cured of a fever; the impotent man at Bethesda is healed; a dumb demoniac is able to speak; the man with palsy regains his health; a woman with an issue of blood recovers her strength (Mk. 1:23–45). While we do not know all the details related to each of these cases, they approximate what we today call "functional ailments." In such events the illness of the body is caused by the sickness of the mind, and vice versa. They fall under the classification of "psychosomatic" cases, where the "mind-body" relation appears in its sensitive interplay. Fear and selfishness so distort the mind, that the physical power of the body is consumed; resentment, suspicion, anger, jealousy, guilt sap the energy of the total self. Physical and mental exhaustion result.

A wholesome use of the Christian religion is an avenue by which the resources of power can be recovered. Says Alexis Carrel, devout Roman Catholic and renowned member of the Rockefeller Institute for Medical Research:

> *Prayer is not only worship; it is also an invisible emanation of man's worshipful spirit—the most powerful form of energy that one can generate. The influence of prayer on the human mind and body is as demonstrable as that of secreting glands. Its results can be measured in terms of increased physical buoyancy, a greater intellectual vigor, moral stamina, and a deeper understanding of the realities underlying human relationships. . . . Prayer is a force*

as real as terrestrial gravity. As a physician I have seen men, after all therapy had failed, lifted out of disease and melancholy by the serene effort of prayer. It is the only power in the world that seems to over-come the so-called "laws of nature"; the occasions on which prayer has dramatically done this have been termed "miracles." But a constant, quieter miracle takes place hourly in the hearts of men and women who have discovered that prayer supplies them with a steady flow of sustaining power in their daily lives. . . . We derive most power from prayer when we use it, not as a petition, but as a supplica-tion that we may become like Him. Prayer should be regarded as practice of the Presence of God.[1]

Jesus was able to bring some of his followers into this "practice of the presence of God," so that they shared His power in their lives. We have a limited amount of energy for our creative living. If we use our first-rate energy in jealousies, suspicions, censoriousness, hatreds, animosities, resentments, then only our second-rate energy remains for our constructive areas of living. The in-sights of Jesus arouse us to our spiritual senses and make us realize the folly of living resentfully (and without power): "Love your enemies and pray for those who persecute you. . . . If you forgive men their trespasses, your heavenly Father will also forgive you. . . . Forgive seventy times seven. . . . Judge not that you be not

[1] "Prayer Is Power," *Reader's Digest*, 1941.

judged. . . . <u>Overcome evil with good</u>." Practising these teachings guides a Christian to power!

Dr. Leslie Weatherhead tells of a woman of ability in an English parish who gradually <u>became ill and was lost</u> to community leadership. Her doctor of medicine was unable to bring her back to health, and solicited the aid of Dr. Weatherhead. After conversations with her, Dr. Weatherhead discovered what he thought might be the cause of her illness: She <u>had</u> quarreled with <u>her brother</u> over some petty grievance. Although the difficulty was small at the start, she <u>brooded over the estrangement</u> so deeply that it soon absorbed her and tired her greatly, causing her illness. Dr. Weatherhead suggested that she <u>invite her brother to tea, tell him of her sorrow over their quarrel and seek his forgiveness.</u> This she did, and within a few weeks she began to gather her former energy; before long she was back again in her role of community and church leadership.

<u>Jesus' spiritual insights</u> show us <u>the secret of the "miracle of Recovery</u>," helping us to realize the truth of Bruce Moore's words:

> *Ah! let Him stand as having power*
> *In some sure place, in some sure hour.*

The late H. G. Wells once said <u>of Jesus:</u> "He is too big for our small hearts." But as we explore this bigness of Jesus, and <u>apply his spiritual suggestions</u> to our tiny lives, we begin <u>to realize</u> that he has the <u>secret to enable us to</u> "<u>stand as having power.</u>"

✥ 12 ✥

THY KINGDOM, LORD, WE LONG FOR

IN 1938, Margaret Slattery wrote a book by the title, *Thy Kingdom Come—But Not Now*. Hurriedly the book went into new editions, partly because of its content by a well-known writer, but partly because of its alluring title. Some people pray weekly, if not daily, "Thy Kingdom come"—but underneath they petition, "but not now," since they are not willing to sacrifice certain habits and things necessary to allow the Kingdom to come. Before his conversion to Christianity, Augustine prayed, "Give me chastity, but do not give it yet." After his conversion, when he prayed, "Thy Kingdom come," he was able to write, "We make a ladder of our vices, if we trample those same vices underfoot." He then viewed the Kingdom as the "City of God."

There was a sense of "frantic immediacy" about Jesus' preaching concerning the Kingdom: "The kingdom of God is *at hand!*" One of the great Jewish prayers of Jesus' time contained this hope: "May He establish His kingdom during your life and during your days." The prophets of Judaism looked for the Kingdom to come within history, for at least the last generation of mankind to receive. During several centuries immediately preceding the era of Jesus, some religious interpreters believed that God would intervene in the present order of events

56

on a resurrection day to give His Kingdom to the faithful. What was a future hope among Jewish interpretations preceding the first century, became a present realization in the insights of Jesus. Said Jesus: "The Kingdom of God has come upon you. . . . If I by the finger of God cast out demons, then the Kingdom of God has come upon you (Lk. 11:20). . . . Blessed are the eyes that see what you see; for I tell you that many prophets and kings wished to see what you see, and did not see it, and to hear what you hear, and did not hear it (Lk. 10:23)."

That which the prophets desired is now a present experience in Jesus' teachings. John the Baptist is the dividing line: before him were the prophets with their hope for the Kingdom; and after him are Jesus and the Kingdom. "The law and the prophets were until John; since then the good news of the kingdom is preached, and every one enters it violently (Lk. 16:16)." While Jesus looks for the completion of the Kingdom in the future, his great stress is on the note: "The Kingdom *has come!*"

In this era following World War II, when some are wondering if civilization will persist, many ponder about the words of Jesus, "Thy kingdom come." Others realize that one of the basic reasons for the downfall of Western culture is that our petition for centuries, "Thy kingdom come," has been immediately followed by a careless, "but not now." Toynbee says that of the sixteen major civilizations which have been demolished, thirteen were destroyed from within by their decline of morality; they committed moral suicide. The safest guarantee today that Western culture will not go "the way of all flesh" is to have men and women pray "Thy kingdom come"—and then go out to live the prayer now!

The secret of God's Kingdom coming now is beautifully described in the words of Vida D. Scudder:

Thy Kingdom, Lord, we long for,
Where Love shall find its own;
And brotherhood triumphant
Our years of pride disown.
Thy captive people languish
In mill and mart and mine:
We lift to thee their anguish.
We wait thy promised sign.[1]

In similar tone Bishop G. Bromley Oxnam in *Look* magazine shows that one of the ways by which America can avert communism is by making its social order more Christian. But first of all each individual must pray, "Thy Kingdom God I long for within myself"; then the individual must join groups who want the Kingdom to come within society. "By their fruits you shall know them."

Dr. Reinhold Niebuhr said at the dedicatory service of the Memorial Chapel at the University of Chicago: "A beautiful chapel has been erected here for our worship. The test of its worship-value will be found in the

[1] From "The Kingdom of God" by Vida D. Scudder. Reprinted by permission of the author.

58

way by which we leave its doors to go out and create a
beautiful world!") For the world, and for ourselves, may
our prayer not be, "Thy kingdom come—but not now."
Rather may it be, "Thy kingdom come in me this day as
it was in Christ!" Perhaps our social prayer will not have
the optimism of the Student Volunteer Movement in
my college days: "The Kingdom of God for the World
in our generation." Yet it must retain the future hope
for the completion of God's Kingdom on this tiny
planet—even though it takes a billion years!)

⟨⟨ 13 ⟩⟩

JESUS, ARTIST OF THE PARABLE

ONE OF the leading contemporary laborers for Zion-
ism is Rabbi Joseph Klausner. From his pen has
come one of the most important books on Jesus, *Jesus
of Nazareth*, written in the Hebrew language, in 1922,
for the Jewish people. In speaking of Jesus he says:

> *Jesus was a great artist in parable. His parables
> are attractive, short, popular, drawn from everyday
> life, full of "instruction in wise conduct," simple
> and profound at the same time—simple in form
> and profound in substance. . . . Jesus was, in popular
> opinion, different from the Pharisees and Scribes
> in that he used allegory and parable instead of
> Scriptural exposition. Jesus was a poet and skilful*

59

story-teller and, therefore, he made use of poetical
descriptions (drawn from everyday life, and, like the
best story-tellers and moral preachers of all times
and races, he unconsciously raised such descriptions
to the level of ethical symbolism.[1]

Many of Jesus parables came from his observance of
nature. Moses saw the burning bush, and realized that
God who designs nature also guides men and women.
Jeremiah looked out upon the almond tree, and felt that
God also shapes the lives of those who are obedient to
Him. Brother Lawrence in the seventeenth century
looked upon a leafless tree, knowing that before long
spring would bring blossoms and leaves to the tree—and
then his thoughts turned to the wonders of God, which
caused his conversion. Jesus, like these sensitive religious
persons, drew lessons from nature, and then applied them
to human experience. He assumed that there was a close
relation between the natural order and the spiritual
order; man and nature are a part of the same universe.

In the mustard seed Jesus saw, through nature, the
mystery of God's growth, active also in the life of man
(Mk. 4:30–32). The mystery was heightened, since in
Jewish thought the Kingdom of God was ever a future
hope; and now Jesus viewed it as a present fact (Mt.
13:24–30). Seeing the sifting of the wheat and tares at
harvest time, Jesus taught that God carries on a winnow-
ing process, in which men decide for or against Him;

[1] Joseph Klausner, *Jesus of Nazareth* (New York: The Macmillan Co.,
1929), pp. 411, 265.

God's judgment is like a time of harvest. Happenings in nature reminded Jesus as to how God touches the life of men. With mystic beauty Jesus agreed that:

In wonder-workings, or some bush aflame,
Men look for God and fancy him concealed;
But in earth's common things he stands revealed
While grass and flowers and stars spell out his name.[2]

In common objects of everyday experience, Jesus saw other spiritual lessons. Observing how freshly pressed, fermenting wine would expand and break an old, fully stretched wineskin, Jesus realized that his forceful, prophetic teaching could not be contained in the old, static receptacle of Pharisaic ritualism (Mk. 2:22). Noticing how a new, unshrunk patch, sewed onto a shrunk piece of cloth, would tear the cloth, he saw that he had not come as a religious reformer to patch up the old Temple system (Mk. 2:21). Seeing a shepherd risk his life to save a sheep caught on a crag, Jesus looked upon God as One who was with His mercy seeking to save a lost sinner (Lk. 15:4–7). Viewing a farmer who sold all his land in order to buy a field in which a treasure is hidden, Jesus looked upon the Kingdom of God as a treasure worth all one's sacrifices (Mt. 13:44). Watching a fisherman seine his fish, with the small ones sifting through the dragnet, Jesus viewed God's judgment of men as going on in the world (Mt. 13:47–50). Seeing a father run out to greet his repentant prodigal son

[2] From "Earth's Common Things" by Minot J. Savage.

Jesus interpreted God as a loving Father whose generous love is ever reaching toward man in his repentance and faith (Lk. 15:11–32).

While Jesus' parables illustrate what the Kingdom of God is like, they are also invitations or "teasers" for people "to come into the Kingdom." In his parables Jesus described the roots and the fruits of religion—"to love thy God" and "to love thy neighbor as thyself." Some years ago a friend of mine was taken by Luther Burbank to view the giant redwood trees. Pointing to a redwood tree, 364 feet in height and 12½ feet in diameter, Burbank said, "That tree was a sappling about the time of Moses. The reason that it has lived so long, and has risen so high, is caused by its roots. As the redwood tree deeply sinks its roots, these roots reach out for the roots of other redwood trees. Thus each tree in its rootage helps to support the other trees. Hence the redwood trees can reach great heights."

As I heard this parable, told by Luther Burbank, and how it taught a great moral-religious lesson, I remembered Jesus as "the artist of the parable"; and that especially his own life was a living parable of his central theme: "The time has reached fulfilment, and the kingdom of God has drawn near. Repent and believe the Gospel." Good news for his day, and for our time as well!

MY ONE UNCHANGED OBSESSION

My one unchanged obsession
Wherever my feet have trod
Is a keen, enormous, haunting
Never-sated thirst for God.[1]

IN THESE words Gamaliel Bradford expresses the deep
hunger of "everyman" for God, including you and
me—certainly including Jesus who calls God "Father."
(This title for God is on Jesus' lips 153 times in the
gospels.) In his Gifford Lectures, given in Edinburgh,
Scotland, in 1902, William James expresses pity for persons who do not believe in God, especially as those individuals move into old age. "Old age," he says, "has the
last word: the purely naturalistic look at life, however
enthusiastically it may begin, is sure to end in sadness.
This sadness lies at the heart of every merely positivistic,
agnostic, or naturalistic scheme of philosophy." One of
the ways out of our spiral in present-day religion is for
people to obtain a faith in God as secure as that which
Jesus possessed.

The Jewish-Christian tradition is almost four thousand years old, running from Abraham through Moses,
Elijah, Hosea, Isaiah, Jeremiah, Jesus, and Paul, through

[1] From "God," *Shadow Verses*, by Gamaliel Bradford. Reprinted by
permission of Yale University Press, publishers.

the church fathers, philosophers, and reformers of the
last nineteen Christian centuries. As every field of knowledge has slowly unraveled its data, so God's revelation
of His character to man has been a gradual unfolding in
the Bible. Many of Jesus' insights about God are similar
to those of the (Hebrew prophets) Hosea taught the
mercy and forgiveness of God as freely given to the repentant; Jesus stressed the redemptive love of God
which pours out upon the undeserving, the unlovely, the
needy, the sinful illustrated in the parables of the prodigal son, the lost sheep, the lost coin) (Lk. 15:2–32);
Jeremiah taught the "new covenant," (in which God and
the individual commune within each person's inner self;)
Jesus taught that "the kingdom of God is within" (Lk.
17:21). Jesus saw God's kingdom, not as something we
build, but as that which God gives to us, as in the parable
of the laborers in the vineyard (Mt. 20:1–16).

God for Jesus was awesome and majestic. Isaiah
viewed God as holy; Jesus looked upon him as "the Lord
of heaven and earth" (Mt. 11:25), the expanse of
heaven is "the throne of God" (Mt. 23:22). Second
Isaiah viewed God as the Lord of all nations; Jesus dis-
cerned him as a universal deity of all mankind [see the
parables of the good Samaritan (Lk. 10:29–37) and the
ten lepers (Lk. 17:11–19), which illustrate that he who
shows mercy toward his neighbor is worthy of God's
kingdom]]

While our "one unchanged obsession" today is a thirst
for God, we sometimes raise the question amid our per-

plexing problems, "What on earth is God doing?" A person who answered this question during World War II replied, "God is holding the moral structure of the universe together. We are reaping in war what we have sown in hatred and selfishness. God is suffering with us in our trouble, giving his energy, mercy, and wisdom to those of us who turn to him for help. God is using our mistakes and our heartaches for some future good, employing those who seek His will as emissaries for some future betterment of the world."

It is still the Christian's answer. Such a hope is to be found in Jesus' teachings: "Everyone who hears these words of mine and does them will be like a wise man who built his house upon the rock; and the rain fell, and the floods came, and the winds blew and beat upon that house, but it did not fall, because it had been founded upon the rock (Mt. 7:24, 25)." Both Jesus and we believe that God is still in control of His universe; He is never to be defeated!

During the American Revolution while Benjamin Franklin was seeking aid from France for the American colonies, he visited the aged Voltaire in Paris. On this visit Voltaire was asked to bless Franklin's grandson, who served as his secretary. Placing his hands on the youth's head, Voltaire said: "My child, God and liberty! Recollect those two words!" Today, as the Christian lives in a world of competing ideologies, let him remember those words—God and liberty! They resound the spirit of Jesus; they are basically involved in the Chris-

65

tian's hope for this world's becoming God's Kingdom.
They alone can satisfy him who has

> *A keen, enormous, haunting*
> *Never-sated thirst for God.*

❧ 15 ❧

WHY ARE MEN RELIGIOUS?

A<small>T</small> Northwestern University Professor Charles S.
Braden and a class in religion sent a questionnaire
to twenty-five hundred people of different backgrounds,
cultures, and religious viewpoints. The questionnaire
listed sixty-five reasons for religious motivation, and was
entitled, "Why People Are Religious." In the compila-
tion of answers the following ten were the primary
reasons for being religious:

(1) *Gives meaning to life*
(2) *Motivates human kindness*
(3) *Provides help in time of stress*
(4) *Enriches life*
(5) *Furnishes a moral ideal*
(6) *Compels one to believe in a supreme being*
(7) *Because of early training*
(8) *Furnishes an aim and purpose for being*
(9) *Gives guidance*
(10) *Makes life worth living*

Jesus considered religion as normal as breathing, eating, and sleeping. To be irreligious was abnormal. "It is your Father's good will to *give* you the kingdom (Lk. 12:32)," said Jesus. It was not something to be *earned*, but a gift to *receive*. "Whosoever shall not receive the kingdom of God as a little child, shall in no wise enter therein (Mk. 10:15)." In the Gospel of John meaningful abundant *life* is shown as the reward for faithfully religious persons: "I am come that ye may have *life*, and have it abundantly (Jn. 10:10)," are the words on Jesus' lips. For Jesus,

> *Religion's all or nothing; it's no mere smile*
> *O' contentment, sigh or aspiration, sir—*
> *No quality o' the finelier-tempered clay*
> *Like its whiteness or its lightness; rather stuff*
> *O' the very stuff, life of life, and self of self.*[1]

One day in discussing the reasons for being religious, Jesus told the story of the tax collector and the Pharisee:

> *Two men went up into the temple to pray, one a Pharisee and the other a tax collector. The Pharisee stood and prayed thus with himself, 'God, I thank thee that I am not like other men, extortioners, unjust, adulterers, or even like this tax collector. I fast twice a week, I give tithes of all that I get.' But the tax collector, standing afar off, would not even lift up his eyes to heaven, but beat his breast, saying, 'God, be merciful to me a sinner!' [Which of these*

[1] From "Religion" by Robert Browning.

men was religious?] I tell you, this man went down to his house justified rather than the other; for every one who exalts himself will be humbled, but he who humbles himself will be exalted.

Like Amos, Hosea, and James, Jesus saw the hypocrisy of substituting ritual for social justice. Cried out Amos: "Let judgment run down as waters and righteousness as a mighty stream (Amos 5:24)." Micah defined religion thus: "What doth the Lord require of thee, but to do justly, and to love mercy, and to walk humbly with thy God (Micah 6:8)." James saw religion in these terms: "Pure religion and undefiled before God and the Father is this—to visit the fatherless and widows in their affliction, and to keep himself unspotted from the world (James 1:27)."

We, like Jesus and the prophets, want religion to cover the entire area of experience. We want a religion of great depth, height, and breadth. Recently in canvassing a gamut of religious interpreters, I found a width of definitions. I am sure that Jesus would have appreciated each person's concept of religion. Here are some of the definitions:

ALFRED NORTH WHITEHEAD: *Religion is what the individual does with his solitariness.* (Jesus was alone in the wilderness, in Gethsemane, on Mt. Olivet.)

FRIEDRICH SCHLEIERMACHER: *Religion is man's feeling of absolute dependence upon God.* (Jesus prayed

"Thy will be done"; "Into Thy hands I commend my spirit.")

EUSTACE HAYDON: *Religion is the co-operative quest for a completely satisfying life.* ("Love your neighbor as yourself," taught Jesus.)

WILLIAM E. HOCKING: *Religion is the habitual reference of life to divine powers.* (Jesus in the gospels refers to God as 'Father' 153 times.)

HARALD HÖFFDING: *The innermost tendency of all religions is the conservation of values.* (Jesus asked, "For what does it profit a man, to gain the whole world and forfeit his life?")

IMMANUEL KANT: *Religion is the recognition of all duties as divine commands.* (Jesus said, "Not every one who says to me 'Lord, Lord,' shall enter the kingdom of heaven, but he who does the will of my Father who is in heaven.")

Jesus was a "religion-intoxicated" person. Religion touched every aspect of his experience all the time. When men follow his religious insights today they find themselves "at home in the universe." Like Walt Whitman Jesus sensed "the necessity of religion":

I say the whole earth, and all the stars in the sky,
are for Religion's sake.
I say no man has ever yet been half devout enough;
None has ever yet adored or worship'd enough;

69

None has begun to think how divine he himself is,
    and how certain the future is.
I say the real and permanent of These States must
    be their Religion;
Otherwise there is no real and permanent grandeur:
(Nor character, nor life worthy the name, without
    Religion;
Nor land, nor man or woman, without Religion.)[2]

Says C. H. Dodd about Jesus' religion: "The decisions at which Jesus arrived in their fundamental principles, hold good against all lapse of time. When moral and religious advance is made, it presents itself as a fresh unfolding as to what Jesus meant."[3] The more men follow Jesus, the more they realize why they are religious.

⋘ 16 ⋙

WHAT IS THE ETHIC OF JESUS?

A SMALL girl had learned the books of the Bible in chronological order from Genesis through Revelation. On being asked to repeat the order of the books before a crowd of people, she replied, "The Bible begins with Genesis and ends with *Revolution!*" Not very good factual scholarship, but excellent biblical theology, for

[2] From "The Necessity of Religion" by Walt Whitman.
[3] *The Authority of the Bible* (New York: Harper and Bros., 1929), p. 282.

when a person really understands the ethic of Jesus, and applies it to himself, a "revolution" occurs in his life!

It was said of the first-century followers of Jesus: "These men have turned the world upside down!" A study of the great personalities of the past and the present shows how the ethic of Jesus becomes a "revolution" in their lives: Augustine, Luther, Wesley, George Fox, John Woolman, Catherine of Genoa, E. Stanley Jones, Albert Schweitzer, Muriel Lester, Toyohiko Kagawa are but a few examples of "revolutionized" lives.

The ethic of Jesus is a religious ethic. Out of right relationship with God, man finds the personal power, wisdom, and love to live with himself, and in right relationship with his fellow men. Dr. Halford Luccock was met by a student's remark: "Religion is all moonshine; and the idea of God is all moonshine!" To which Dr. Luccock replied: "I agree. Have you ever been to Panama at the time of a full moon, where the moonshine pulls up billions of tons of water because of a twenty-two-foot tide? The moonshine shows the pull of another world, unseen but resistless in force. God is like that; He is unseen but resistless in His pull upon the life of man!"

In her vivid way Evelyn Underhill further expresses the pattern for the ethic of Jesus: "To do great things for souls, you must become the agent and channel of a more than human love; and this must be the chief object of a priest's life in prayer. It means a most careful preservation of our Lord's balance between solitary communion with the Father and loving-spending with man."

71

Various interpretations have been made of the ethic of Jesus: (1) Some view Jesus' ethic as a way to save the individual out of the sinful world, (to make him ready for a judgment day which Jesus' return will inaugurate) Not long ago a minister and his flock in California started fasting for twenty-four hours, as they awaited the return of Jesus to initiate the end of the world. (2) Others feel that the monastic life is the highest way to practise the ethic of Jesus. Those who live the hard disciplines of the monasteries feel that they are saving themselves from the world into the eternal *City of God;* and at the same time they are effecting salvation for other believers. (3) Still others look upon the ethic of Jesus as a set of ethical rules, especially found in the Sermon on the Mount (Mt. 5–7), by which men are to *build* the Kingdom of God on earth. (By applying Jesus' personal teachings to ourselves, we can have mental health; and (by joining Jesus-like social movements, we can improve society. (Since so many of Jesus' ethical teachings are similar to those of other religions—such as Buddhism, Zoroastrianism, Judaism, Confucianism—this view would add to Christianity little that is unique.) (4) Recent theological attitudes, especially strong in Wesern Europe, view man as so sinful that he can in no way do anything with Jesus' ethic to bring the Kingdom of God on earth. One of these European theologians said a few years ago: "If the Kingdom of God is ever to come on earth, there is not a single thing that man can do about it. It will be *entirely a gift of God.*")

The ethic of Jesus is concerned with *what* can be done for the world. But it is also concerned with *who* can do it. Jesus illustrated in his parable of the laborers in the vineyard (Mt. 20:1–16), that the Kingdom is God's *gift* to those who are willing to receive it through their faith and repentance. The universe is God's Kingdom: men are to receive it from God, and live it among their fellow men. A woman recently expressed this view:

> The eyes of my soul were opened, and I beheld the fulness of God. So that through excess of marvelling my soul cried out with a loud voice, saying: *This whole world is full of God! and I understood how small a thing the whole world is—the abyss, the ocean, and all things, and how the power of God exceeds and fills all!*

Jean-Baptiste-Marie Vianney (1788–1859), the Cure d'Ars, pattern and patron saint of parish priests, illustrates how one lives the ethic of Jesus: Though limited by his humble origins and intellectual power, he possessed a maximum of devotedness to God and man. He spent his whole life ministering to what was called a hopeless French village. He spent sixteen hours a day ministering to troubled souls, his Church becoming a place of pilgrimage for all France. Spending much time each day in deep, personal intercourse with God, his life shared his power, wisdom, and love; as his life was transformed by communion with God, he in turn transformed his French community. He found the secret of the real ethic of Jesus: "It means a most careful preservation of our Lord's balance between solitary communion with the Father and loving self-spending with men!"

❧ 17 ❧

THE CREED OF CHRIST—OUR JUDGMENT AND OUR HOPE

MAHATMA GANDHI did not hold to Christian theology; yet he believed that the Sermon on the Mount (Mt. 5–7) was the world's highest ethical code—and he abided by it. Joseph Klausner, Palestinian rabbi, speaks of these teachings as "one of the choicest treasures in the literature of Israel for all time." Thomas W. Manson, Bible scholar of Manchester University, England, says that the Sermon on the Mount gives "a number of illustrations of the way in which a transformed character will express itself in conduct."

Look at the beauty and the depth of "the creed of Christ":

> *Blessed are the poor in spirit...those who mourn ...the meek...those who hunger and thirst for righteousness...the merciful...the peacemakers... those who are persecuted for righteousness' sake... You are the salt of the earth...You are the light of the world...everyone who is angry with his brother shall be liable to judgment...everyone who looks at*

a woman lustfully has already committed adultery
with her in his heart...Do not resist one who is
evil...Love your enemies and pray for those who
persecute you...You must be perfect as your heav-
enly Father is perfect...Beware of practising your
piety before men in order to be seen of them...You
cannot serve God and mammon...Do not be anx-
ious about your life . . . Judge not that ye be not
judged...(From Mt. 5–7).

"The Sermon on the Mount," says E. Stanley Jones,
"is the transcript of Jesus' mind and spirit. It commands
our reverence and respect, but more—it commands our
obedience and our very all. It is a working philosophy of
life—the only one that will work, for the universe backs
this way of life."[1]

The first disciples of Jesus held similar confidence in
it as a way of life. His followers looked upon the Sermon
on the Mount as the "new Law." The "old Law" had
been given Israel through Moses on Mount Sinai; the
"new Law" had been revealed on the mountain through
Jesus to the "new Israel" (the Christians). Before Jesus'
death the teachings of the Sermon on the Mount showed
how men must act if they are to receive the gift of God's
Kingdom. After Jesus' resurrection this creed showed how
Christians must adapt themselves to the problems of life.
Because *Jesus* spoke these teachings, many of them ages
old, Christians looked upon this "sermon" as God's eter-

[1] *The Christ of the Mount* (New York: Abingdon-Cokesbury Press,
1931), pp. 331, 332.

75

nal will which they must obey. "He taught them as one having authority."

"But how can I be expected to keep all these teachings!" exclaims a thoughtful Christian. "They are too absolute, too impossible for one like me to obey." Martin Dibelius, wise German scholar, helps answer the question:

> *The Sermon on the Mount makes demands too exacting to be fulfilled in life on this earth. The Sermon on the Mount must be taken seriously as an expression of the divine will—even in this world. Yet the commandments of the Sermon on the Mount cannot be fully performed in this age.*[2]

I remember seeing Tolstoy's play, *Light Shining in Darkness,* in Giessen, Germany, some years ago. It is the story of Nicolai Ivanovitsch Sarynzev, who attempts to live by the Sermon on the Mount. He rids himself of his property; he attempts to earn his living as a joiner; he causes his daughter's fiancé to revolt against army service; he brings unhappiness to his family. He finds that the Sermon on the Mount taken literally and radically is not practical in the world. Perhaps so! Yet it is the direction toward which transformed Christian characters should be living. Even though we cannot *perform* all its precepts, it will *transform* us. It is a "design for living," a set of plans toward which our building ("not made with hands") should be progressing.

[2] *The Sermon on the Mount* (New York: Charles Scribner's Sons, 1940), p. 101.

Jesus' followers bel_
_own creed. "The man
tised them, and the pra
acter so beautiful, so co_
to be, that he is as inesca
force of gravity is in the p
trates how we *ought* to liv
It also acts as *a judgment*
from its teachings or fail to
feel ourselves under its critic
gave his disciples," says Arcl   so
much a new law as a design fo   He set them,
as He sets us, an ideal to aim at, and a standard to judge
themselves by."[3]

Perhaps it is more "the Christ on the Mount" than the
"Sermon on the Mount") that makes the "sermon" mem-
orable. As it was said of Saint Francis, so was it said of
Jesus:

> *Saint Francis came to preach. With smiles he met*
> *The friendless, fed the poor, freed a trapped bird,*
> *Led home a child. Although he spoke no word,*
> *His text, God's love, the town did not forget.*[4]

What Jesus said and how he lived were one, in the memories of his friends!

[3] *The Work and Words of Jesus* (Westminster Press, 1950), p. 66.
[4] From "Sermon Without Words" by Elizabeth Patton Moss.

18

CAN RELIGION BRING US HAPPINESS?

IN THE summer of 1949 a group of eighteen people met for fifteen hours over a weekend at the Westchester Country Club in Rye, New York, to discuss the theme, "Can Religion Bring Us Happiness?" Some of those present were: Father Edmund Walsh, Georgetown University; Sidney Hook, professor of philosophy, New York University; Theodore Green, professor of philosophy, Princeton University; Erich Fromm, writer; Stuart Chase, writer on economic problems; Charles Brackett, Hollywood producer; Henry R. Luce, editor of *Time, Life,* and *Fortune;* Mrs. Herbert Hines, mother of the year 1948; Betsey Barton, writer, who lost the use of her legs in 1935 in an auto crash. Casual statements from their discussion are:

> *Happiness is possible as one is able to relate oneself to the world, in love and thought. . . . Religious faith has more to do with happiness for the individual than anything else. . . . Self-sacrifice is necessary for happiness. . . . Happiness is an inner state, an inner achievement. . . . Suffering and pain are the greatest character builders; suffering is not good in itself, but it shifts our expectation for happiness from without to within.*

Nineteen hundred years ago Jesus assembled a group of his friends, and gave them identical suggestions for happiness. He told them that self-sacrifice is necessary for happiness: The greatest of all is a servant . . . he who loses his life for my sake and the gospel's will save it . . . greater love has no man than this that a man lay down his life for his friends One of his evangelists catalogued Jesus' guides to happiness in eight beatitudes:

> Blessed are the poor in spirit, for theirs is the
> kingdom of heaven.
> Blessed are those who mourn, for they shall be
> comforted.
> Blessed are the meek, for they shall inherit the
> earth.
> Blessed are those who hunger and thirst after
> righteousness, for they shall be satisfied.
> Blessed are the merciful, for they shall obtain
> mercy.
> Blessed are the pure in heart, for they shall see
> God.
> Blessed are the peacemakers, for they shall be
> called sons of God.
> Blessed are those who are persecuted for
> righteousness' sake, for theirs is the
> kingdom of heaven. (Mt. 5:3–10)

Getting at the basis of Jesus' secret of happiness, Eugene O'Neill, American playwright, says if the human

79

race is so stupid that in two thousand years it hasn't had brains enough to appreciate that the secret of happiness is in one simple statement it ought to perish. Even a school kid can understand it. It is this: "What shall it profit a man if he gain the whole world and lose his own soul." At the heart of Jesus' insights into life, happiness is not something one goes in search of, but a *by-product* of a life which has lost itself in the interests of other persons.

Ralph W. Sockman speaks of Jesus' beatitudes as insights into "The Higher Happiness":

> *The Beatitudes run so counter to the current of the ideas of happiness that men find them hard to believe. Some would explain them as applying only to that perfect kingdom which is to be consummated at the end of history. But as Toynbee reminds us, "the divine 'Other World' transcends the earthly life of man without ceasing to include it." Since "the Kingdom of God is within you" as well as a future consummation, its rules have a relevance here and now.[1]*

There is a grave conflict between the worldly and the Christian conceptions of happiness. Amid the pomp of the French court of Louis XIV, a court preacher named Massillon included these poignant words in a sermon to the king:

[1] *The Higher Happiness* (Abingdon-Cokesbury Press, 1950), p. 12.

If the world addressed your majesty from this place, the world would not say, "Blessed are they that mourn," but "Blessed is the prince who has never fought but to conquer; who has filled the universe with his name; who through the whole course of a long and flourishing reign enjoys in splendor all that men admire—extent of conquest, the esteem of enemies, the love of his people, the wisdom of his laws." But, sire, the language of the gospel is not the language of the world.

Is there any wonder that the preacher of the court could find only four words in eulogy at the burial service for Louis XIV, "Only God is great!" Neither greatness nor happiness were defined by Jesus in terms of conquest, but in terms of service. As Jesus died upon a cross a centurion soldier near by eulogized him in these words, "Truly this man was the son of God!"

A poll recently questioned the happiness of Americans. Forty-six per cent of those polled said they were very happy; forty-five per cent were fairly happy; nine per cent were unhappy. Yet in this country fourteen million are suffering from serious mental illness; seven million are in mental hospitals; one half of our hospital beds are used for psychiatric cases. There is still wide room for the Christian religion with its key to happiness to play a major role in American life!

19

WHERE I LOVE, I LIVE

IN RECENT years two universities in Sweden, Uppsala and Lund, have made rich interpretations of Christian love, showing how it differs from other ideas of love. One major writing in three volumes by Anders Nygren, professor of theology at Lund, is titled *Agape and Eros*. These terms from the Greek language have become words with a common English usage. *Eros* is a selfish love which a person has for an object; he feels he can obtain value from that which he "loves": a play which you see, a book which you read, a friend whom you appreciate are all objects from which you get value. A friend of mine once said to me, "I frequently listen to 'Liebestod' from *Tristan and Isolde*, since I get so much from it—just to hear it gives me a new feel of courage. I am then able to hold my head a bit higher and my shoulders a bit more erect!" A literary acquaintance said to me several years ago, "I am reading once again on my train travels, Shakespeare's plays. I get something from them which gives me deep insights into my own problems." Each of these persons in his "selfish" interests possessed *Eros*.

One can also have *Eros*—a selfish love—toward God. Isaac Watts' great hymn based on Psalm 90 depicts this kind of love:

> *O God, our help in ages past;*
> *Our hope for years to come;*
> *Be Thou our God while troubles last,*
> *And our eternal home.*

Eliza Scudder shows the same human desire for God:

> *I cannot lose Thee! Still in Thee abiding,*
> *The end is clear, how wide soe'er I roam;*
> *The Hand that holds the worlds my steps is guiding,*
> *And I must rest at last in Thee, my home.*[1]

The way in which *Eros* is used determines whether a person is a Christian or a pagan: a pagan gets what he can through his selfish desires for his own private ends; while a Christian improves his selfish desires, so that his personality has more to give to those who are in need. A Christian, however, possesses an added type of love for helping others; it is called *Agape,* which signifies a love unselfishly poured out upon the undeserving, the unlovely, the unattractive. It is the kind of love which helps the weakness and need of other people and their environments. *Eros* wishes to *get* value for oneself; *Agape* wishes to *give* value to others.

I recently read of a woman living in a New York tenement house: when her widowed neighbor across the hall died, leaving seven children, she took them into her flat, although she had to work nights as a scrubwoman in

[1] From "The Quest" by Eliza Scudder. Reprinted by permission of Houghton Mifflin Company, publishers.

83

order to support the orphans. She possessed *Agape*, an unselfish, redemptive love. A college student who, out of his allowance, gave several CARE packages to help needy Europeans, illustrates *Agape*.

Jesus in his parables of the prodigal son, the lost coin, the lost sheep teaches (Lk. 15) that God treats us with *Agape*, an unselfish redemptive love to supplement our human weaknesses; that God forgives us our weaknesses and heals us of our vices as He directs *Agape* toward us. (If a Christian has right relationship with God, then he will act with *Agape* toward his fellowmen and their conditions. Several years ago in Chicago, a study of juvenile delinquency showed the area around the stock yards as one of the worst. After a sociological survey of that area was made, the need for recreational centers and playgrounds was unearthed. These lacks were supplied and after these centers for helping youth had begun to function, the stock-yard area had one of the best records of juvenile behavior. Is this not a social example of how *Agape* functions in a practical way in everyday living?

Paul, the great interpreter of Christ, in a highly inspired moment wrote his *Hymn to Agape* (I Cor. 13): in this hymn he says that *Agape* suffers long, is kind, envies not, seeks not her own, bears all things, is not easily provoked, is not proud, endures all things... *Agape* never fails. Jesus in the Sermon on the Mount (Mt. 5–7) describes the person who possesses *Agape* as one who is humble, merciful, deeply desirous of spiritual growth, pure in heart, willing to forgive men their trespasses, trustful of God's *Agape*, willing to overcome evil with good, desirous of exerting *Agape* not only toward friends but also toward enemies. The writings of John say that God is *Agape*; that God so loved the world that he *gave* his only begotten son. Like the theme recurring in a symphony *Agape* resounds over and over again in the New Testament. The secret of Jesus' incarnation lay in the fact that he possessed *Agape*; His life left the impression so accurately caught by Robert Southwell, "Not where I breathe, but where I love, I live."

❧ 20 ❧

HE SOUGHT THE MOUNTAINS AND THE LONELIEST HEIGHT

E STANLEY JONES has written in a booklet, *How to Pray*, some wise words on the artistry of prayer. In this volume he says:

> Breathe the prayer, "Lord teach us to pray," as you begin the quest for a prayer life. Bathe your very quest in prayer. . . . Another thought that may serve as a background: Prayer is not only the reference of the weak; it is the reinforcement of the strong. . . . Prayer is not bending God to my will, but it is a bringing of my will into conformity with God's will, so that His will may work in and through me. . . . Prayer is not an occasional exercise to which you turn now and then; it is a life attitude. It is the will

to co-operate with God in your total life ... Prayer is primarily and functionally surrender. ... Prayer is secondarily assertion. Two attitudes combine—surrender and assertion. The two have to be together; if you only surrender you are weak; if you only assert you are weak. But if you are surrendered and then assertive, you are really strong. You are going to be a positive creative person because surrendered to the will of God. You are beginning the adventure of co-operation with God. Prayer is just that—co-operation with God.[1]

These words are of great help to modern man who beseeches, "Teach us to pray." Centuries ago, when Jesus' disciples saw what prayer did to him, they made the same request, "Lord, teach us to pray." Prayer was the secret of Jesus' life: Mark tells how Jesus departed early in the morning to pray (Mk. 1:35); late in the evening after teaching the crowds all day he withdrew to the mountain for prayer (Mk. 6:46); before he was arrested he prayed alone (Mk. 14:32); when pressed by the crowds to carry on his healings, he departed for prayer (Lk. 5:16); before he chose his twelve disciples, he prayed (Lk. 6:12); before he asked the disciples their opinion of him, he was in meditation (Lk. 9:18). Jesus' life was so radiant from what he obtained in his consistent praying, that it is no wonder his followers besought him, "Lord, teach us to pray."

[1] *The Christian Advocate.*

Hartley Coleridge catches the vision of "Jesus Praying":

He sought the mountain and the loneliest height,
For He would meet his Father all alone,
And there, with many a tear and many a groan,
He strove in prayer throughout the long, long night.
Why need He pray, who held by filial right,
O'er all the world alike of thought and sense,
The fulness of his Sire's omnipotence?
Why crave in prayer what was his own by might?
Vain is the question—Christ was man in need,
And being man his duty was to pray.
The son of God confess'd the human need,
And doubtless ask'd a blessing every day,
Nor ceases yet for sinful man to plead,
Nor will, till heaven and earth shall pass away.

Gerald Heard mentions three types of persons concerned with prayer: (1) the religious psychologist, who studies prayer as scientifically and objectively as he would a specimen in a biological laboratory, although he himself never prays; (2) the individual who devoutly prays, but who never wishes to make an analytical study of prayers for fear the value of his praying might be lost; (3) the person who makes a scientific study of prayer, and who also prays. The third individual, according to Dr. Heard, is the one who will understand prayer. At Laguna Beach, where Dr. Heard and others have a "College of Prayer," the members of this "college" not only study prayer but also spend time each day in prayer. Hence they are discovering results.

Jesus conducted his "College of Prayer" for his disciples. For their basic lesson he told them to pray thus:

> *Our Father, who art in heaven,*
> *Hallowed be thy name.*
> *Thy kingdom come, thy will be done,*
> *On earth as it is in heaven.*
> *Give us this day our daily bread;*
> *And forgive us our debts,*
> *As we also have forgiven our debtors;*
> *And lead us not into temptation,*
> *But deliver us from evil. . . . (Mt. 6:9–13)*

Based upon lofty prayer ideas of Judaism, this form of the Lord's Prayer so universally used contains the heart of Jesus' prayer insights, framed into a poem for liturgical use. Beginning with adoration of God and ending with contrition of man, it reveals the secret of all great religious contemplation.

We today who want world concord see its secret in the way men worship and pray together. Rabbi Ferdinand M. Isserman tells of a Protestant Episcopal medical doctor saying: "Communion is one of the most hallowed experiences of my life." He sees an aged, poverty-stricken woman with new light in her eyes and vigor in her body as she leaves a Roman Catholic Mass. He views his Jewish friends made better men and women at the Passover. Then he says, "What matters it to God what the form

88

of worship, so long as they know he is one, so long as they think of him as ideal justice and love, so long as they seek to pattern their lives after his nature?"[2]

I am sure that Jesus, who often "sought the mountains and the loneliest height" in prayer, would agree with this wise modern rabbi. And I presume that Jesus in his "College of Prayer" taught such basic truths about prayer. For he knew that for all men,

> *More things are wrought by prayer*
> *Than this world dreams of.*

❧ 21 ❧

HOW CAN I CONQUER MY FEARS?

WILLIAM JAMES once said that people with no abiding philosophy grow in sadness and possess sick souls; their lives are pervaded and poisoned with their fears. Madame Chiang Kai-chek tells of passing from fear to courage as her religious philosophy developed. Before she acquired a stable religious viewpoint she says, "I had no staying power, I was depending on self. I was plunged into dark despair, bleakness, desolation." Then came a cure for her fear and despair: "I entered into the period where I wanted to do, not my will, but God's. I used to pray that God would do this or that. Now I pray only

[2] *This Is Judaism* (New York: Harper and Bros., 1944), p. 216.

that God will make His will known to me. Prayer is a source of guidance and balance. God is able to enlighten the understanding. I am often bewildered, because my mind is only finite. I question and doubt my own judgments. Then I seek guidance, and when I am sure, I go ahead, leaving the results with Him."

Jesus looked upon worry as unnecessary and useless, since God always cares for us. God gave our lives to us; He will sustain us in His universe. Worry is futile, since it neither accomplishes nor escapes any problem. Worry is dangerous, for it takes our attention from trust in God and directs it toward distrust of self—thus it puts self rather than God at the center of our interest. Like the Hebrew prophets, Jesus saw God as One who worked both in nature and in men. Lilies retain their lovely and peaceful beauty, since they respond without antagonism to God's merciful laws of growth. Even wise men like Solomon lack the beauty and peace of nature, because with their human freedom they do not wholeheartedly trust God nor obey his laws. God is unselfish with his love, and will lavish it on us as much as he does on the lilies—if we will only let him.

Jesus said: "Do not be anxious about your life, what you shall eat or what you shall drink, nor what you shall put on. Is not life more than food, and the body more than clothing? Look at the birds of the air: they neither sow nor reap nor gather into barns, and yet your heavenly Father feeds them. Are you not of more value than they? And which of you by being anxious can add one cubit to his span of life? . . . . But seek ye first His Kingdom and His righteousness, and all these things shall be yours as well (Mt. 6:25–34)." Said one person, torn by his fears, "As I prayed and read those words, a miracle happened: my nervous tensions fell away. My anxieties, fears, and worries were transformed into heart-warming courage and hope and triumphant faith."

It is estimated that nine tenths of our worries are subjective, centering about things which will never happen, caused by our being filled with selfishness, fears, resentments, and guilt. Some of us would do well to emulate the woman who realized that her fears were ruining her life, so she made for herself a "worry table." In tabulating her worries, she discovered these figures:

> *40%—will never happen; anxiety is the result of a tired mind,*
> *30%—about old decisions which I cannot alter,*
> *12%—others criticism of me, most untrue, made by people who feel inferior,*
> *10%—about my health, which gets worse as I worry,*
> *8%—"legitimate," since life has some real problems to meet.*

In looking at her "legitimate" worries, she realized a great truth: that when she faced these problems with her own resources, the help of friends, and the aid of God, these experiences deepened her character and developed courage for future events. Hence, through the alleviation of ninety-two per cent of her worries, she realized she could change her life from a state of fear into a state of wonder!

A friend of mine tells of being transported one evening in a rather shoddy private airplane by an unknown pilot. At first he was frightened because he knew little of the ability of the pilot or the condition of the plane. After he had traveled a short distance he discovered a secret by which he could calm his fears while in flight. On the board of the plane in front of the pilot was a number of lights; and my friend discovered that, as the pilot turned his head to the right or the left, he could see the pilot's facial outline silhouetted against the lights. "As long as his face showed no distress," he said, "I realized that there was no reason for me to be afraid." Is there not a parable there for us who today are trying to conquer our fears? Centuries ago there lived one who was called "the Light of the world." He was, in the words of Robert Norwood, "one who always seemed at ease with God." Let us remember that Jesus and we live in the same universe. We, too, through following His trust can be at ease with God.

❧ 22 ❧

A PRESENT HELP IN TROUBLE

IT IS February 23, A.D. 155. A great pagan festival is being held in Smyrna, prominent city in Asia Minor. Before the inflamed crowds, Polycarp (Bishop of

Smyrna) is urged to renounce his Christian beliefs, and thus secure his liberty. With calm spirit, quiet dignity, and unperturbed courage Polycarp replies: "Eighty and six years have I served Him, and He hath done me no wrong. How then can I speak evil of my King who has saved me?" Soon the faggots and timber are placed upon the pyre; Polycarp heroically goes to his martyrdom amidst the roaring flames.

It is shortly before A.D. 70; Christians at Rome have gone through the persecutions of Nero. Many have died as martyrs, burned at the stake or thrown to the lions before the seething crowds of the amphitheater. One day a group of Christians, gathered together in one of their homes at Rome, receive an important document, the Gospel of Mark. As it is read to the group, many of them, frightened by the atmosphere of persecution, take on new courage. The gospel devotes about one half of its content to the passion of Jesus (Mk. 8:31–16:8); and one fifth of its narrative to Jesus' "last week" at a Passover feast, where he went as a courageous martyr to meet his suffering and death. The writer of this gospel has several sentences which especially appeal to the Christians at Rome, though they were spoken to Jesus' disciples forty years earlier, at the beginning of Jesus' last trip to Jerusalem: "If any man would come after me, let him deny himself and take up his cross and follow me. For whoever would save his life will lose it; and whoever loses his life for my sake and the gospel's will save it. For what doth it profit a man, to gain the

whole world and forfeit his life (Mk. 8:34–36)?" Said
one of the leading Christians at Rome, "What Jesus said
to his first disciples, he continues to say to us. His gospel
is still a present help in trouble."

Christianity was not born in easy times; that is why
as a religion it has always appealed to people in difficult
days. It ever shows its adherents that suffering rightly
faced, both *makes* a person something, and *teaches* him
something as well. Carlyle once said that we speak often
about the rights of men; that we ought also to say more
about the strength of men. Christianity rightly speaks
about both the rights and the strength of men. As war-
time teaches us that men by rigorous physical discipline
can stand unimaginable hardships, Christianity likewise
shows us that by spiritual discipline we can face with
God any kind of spiritual difficulty and tribulation.

A favorite story among the Christians at Rome was
about Jesus' quieting the waves: The disciples, frightened by the sudden storm on the sea of Galilee, and the
beating of the waves into the boat, aroused Jesus from
his sleep. On awaking, Jesus said, "Peace! Be still!" And
the wind ceased, and there was a great calm. He said to
them, "Why are you afraid? Have you no faith (Mk.
4:35–41)?" Roman Christians caught the value of this
story: Jesus continued to come to them as a Saviour,
bringing them peace and courage as the waves of Roman
persecution tossed high around them. His gospel continued to be for them a present help in time of trouble.

For eighteen years (1870–1888) Edward Hopper min-

94

istered to the "Church of the Sea and Land" in New York City. His work was especially vital among the sailors. His own life, long afflicted by a weak heart, came to a sudden end while he was seated at his study desk, pencil in hand, writing lines on the theme, "Heaven." In 1871, inspired by the story of Jesus' quieting the waves, and deeply aware of the needs of the mariners to whom he preached, Dr. Hopper wrote these words,

> *Jesus, Saviour, pilot me*
> *Over life's tempestuous sea;*
> *Unknown waves before me roll,*
> *Hiding rock and treacherous shoal;*
> *Chart and compass come from Thee:*
> *Jesus, Saviour, pilot me.*
>
> *As a mother stills her child,*
> *Thou canst hush the ocean wild;*
> *Boisterous waves obey Thy will*
> *When Thou say'st to them, "Be still!"*
> *Wondrous Sovereign of the sea,*
> *Jesus, Saviour, pilot me.*

Many today amid the turbulence of world revolution continue to find solace and quietude as Jesus' religion pilots them "over life's tempestuous sea." In the spirit of the Psalmist they can say:

God is our refuge and strength,
A very present help in trouble.

95

Therefore will not we fear, though the mountains be re-
moved,
Though the mountains be carried into the sea;
Though the waters thereof roar and be troubled,
Though the mountains shake with the swelling thereof.
(Psalm 46)

◆❧ 23 ❧◆

A TRAGIC HOME-COMING

FAMILY PORTRAIT is a play about Jesus by Lenore Coffee and William Cowen. Though Jesus never appears upon the stage, he is constantly in the conversations of the other characters in the drama. Jesus' home-coming at Nazareth is especially of interest: Mary, the mother of Jesus, wants to look her best when Jesus comes back to preach in the home synagogue. She buys a blue scarf from a peddler, to wear for the occasion, remarking to Mary Cleopas, "Oh, dear—maybe I shouldn't! But I *do* want to look my best. Do you think He'll like it?" Hepzibah a neighbor wants to lend dishes to Mary for Jesus' home-coming, so that she may be "in" on the great event. Wondering if Jesus will reside at his own home during the home-coming, she says, "I just thought some prominent people might want to entertain him. . . . Well, if there's anything else you want, just ask for it. It'll be a pleasure. . . ." But after Jesus' sorry home-coming and the rejection of him by his home folks, where the "prophet is not without honor, except in his own country," Hepzibah speaks: "Well, if you ask me, I was glad to see this family put in its place."

The experience of Jesus in his home town (Mk. 6:1–6) well illustrates the wisdom of a Jewish proverb: "No prophet is popular in his native town, and no physician effects cures among his friends." An expert has been defined as "an ordinary person away from home"; but at home he remains "ordinary." One of the problems discussed among the leaders of the first-century Church was: "Why did the Gentiles accept the religion of Jesus, while his Jewish fellowmen rejected him in his home town?" This Nazareth story was the stimulus of that discussion. The human side of Jesus appears in this event: He is the carpenter, the son of Mary and brother of James and Joseph and Judas and Simon, and his sisters are with him. (The Roman Catholic Church believes that Jesus' brothers and sisters are children of a step-mother, Jesus being the only child of Mary.) The gospel writer infers that Jesus is ineffective among the people of Nazareth, since they have no faith in him. Certainly Jesus' return to Nazareth was a tragic home-coming!

We today may not live in Nazareth, but our home towns are similar to Jesus' home town. We, too, either reject him or accept him in our communities. Unless we have a note of belief as to who Jesus is, his effectiveness in our individual and community lives will be nihil. Jesus in no way affected the lives of Pilate and the Sanhedrin, nor did he impress the citizens of Nazareth, since they lacked a note of "faith" that he was bringing God to men in an unusual way.

"*Unfaith*," says Martin Dibelius, "really consists in refusing to discern Jesus as God's actual revelation to us, and dedicating our lives to it. For certainly the future destiny of the race depends in large measure upon the way in which the conflict between faith and unfaith develops. Again and again has come from the story of Jesus the call for decision."[1] The manner in which we respond faithfully to Jesus' way of life in our communities today causes the kind of "home-coming" we afford him.

As John Henry Newman in the nineteenth century went among the villages of England, he noticed in some of them neatly kept yards and attractive homes, children clean and polite, an atmosphere of friendliness among the people. In these noticeably different communities, he asked the people the reason for their fine villages. Invariably would come the answer, "A man by name of John Wesley once came this way and visited us." Is it not in similar fashion that we afford Jesus a proper "home-coming" in our communities, as we become instruments of his spirit in our human relationships?

In the middle of the nineteenth century, Theodore Parker ranked as one of Boston's most provocative preachers, especially concerned with Christianity as a set

[1] *Jesus* (Westminster Press, 1949), p. 146.

98

of vital social attitudes rather than a code of theological
concepts. In his poem, "The Way, the Truth and the
Life," he gives the "eye of faith" as to how we today
can avoid giving Jesus "a tragic home-coming":

O thou great Friend to all the sons of men,
Who once appear'dst in humblest guise below,
Sin to revoke, to break the captive's chain,
To call thy brethren forth from want to woe!
Thee would I sing. Thy truth is still the light
Which guides the nations groping on their way,
Stumbling and falling in disastrous night,
Yet hoping ever for the perfect day.
Yes, thou art still the life; thou art the way
The holiest know—light, life, and way of heaven;
And they who dearest hope and deepest pray
Toil by the truth, life, way that thou hast given;
And in thy name aspiring mortals trust
To uplift their bleeding brothers rescued from the dust.

❦ 24 ❧

DEFEAT MAY SERVE AS WELL AS VICTORY

SEVERAL years ago I visited the medical school at the
University of Pennsylvania, where from a small
clinic amphitheater I observed cases of melancholia and
depression being treated by the doctors. Each of these
persons was an individual who had let a disturbing experience defeat him—hence hospitalization was the re-

sult. Many of the persons could have avoided mental illness had they realized that:

Defeat may serve as well as victory
To shake the soul and let the glory out.
When the great oak is straining in the wind
The boughs drink in new beauty, and the trunk
Sends down a deeper root on the windward side.
Only the soul that knows the mighty grief
Can know the mighty rapture. Sorrows come
To stretch out spaces in the heart for joy.[1]

Jesus' mission in and around Galilee had made a deep impression upon many of his hearers. "All are seeking thee (Mk. 1:37)," his disciples told him after his preaching on a Sabbath at Capernaum. The crowds who came to hear him along the shores of Galilee were so immense that Jesus had to speak to them from a boat (Mk. 3:7–10). Five thousand persons listening to him at another time indicate the popularity of his Galilean ministry (Mk. 6:44). Jesus appealed especially to the common people, who lacked deep loyalty to the ritualistic laws of Judaism. To them Jesus seemed to have a greater authority than the scribes (Mk. 1:22, 27), for his wisdom seemed to come directly from God rather than from the Torah (Law). They were astonished at his wisdom (Mk. 6:2); they were won by his graciousness (Lk. 4:22). Yet Jesus knew that, in spite of the crowds who were at-

[1] From "Victory in Defeat" by Edwin Markham. Reprinted by permission of Virgil Markham.

tracted to his message, others in Galilee were indifferent, shallow, and antagonistic. He compared his message to a seed, and his listeners to types of soil—like unto rocky soil, thorny soil, surface soil, good soil. Jesus' ministry in Galilee was an odd mixture of defeat and victory.

Along with the indifference of many Galileans to Jesus' ministry there was the antagonism of some of the Pharisees. These rigid legalists were more concerned with outer piety than inner religious integrity. Jesus criticised them for their public praying, fasting, and alms-giving which they substituted for righteousness toward their fellowmen (Mt. 6:1–18). "This people," he quoted Isaiah regarding them, "honor me with their lips, but their heart is far from me." Jesus, in disagreement with them, healed a man on the Sabbath, forgave sins, welcomed Samaritans and Gentiles into his Kingdom movement, mingled with sinners and outcasts. Hence, the Pharisees sought to disrupt Jesus' Galilean ministry. Enlisting the enmity of Herod, ruler of Galilee who beheaded John the Baptist, they attempted to bring Jesus' Galilean ministry to an end. The inevitable conflict which was later to bring about Jesus' death at Jerusalem was initially enacted in Galilee.

With the apparent defeat of his work in Galilee, Jesus might easily have quit his Kingdom program—but Jesus was not like that, for he knew that

Defeat may serve as well as victory
To shake the soul and let the glory out.

Perhaps Jesus thought on Habakkuk, the prophet, who spoke to Judah when the Chaldeans were bringing forth their destruction upon her. Though momentarily puzzled as to *why* a cruel nation like the Chaldeans could be victorious, Habakkuk did not *lose* his religion. Rather he *used* his religion, as he sat upon his watchtower, waiting for God's answer and saying, "The righteous man lives by his faithfulness in God." As Jesus faced opposition in Galilee, he too *used* his religion. He lived by his faith in God. He believed the courageous philosophy:

> *Then welcome each rebuff*
> *Which turns earth's smoothness rough;*
> *Each sting that bids not sit, nor stand, but go.*[2]

With Galilee behind him, with its mixture of success and failure, Jesus moved to the region around Caesarea Philippi, where Philip was the ruler. After Peter's confession at Caesarea Philippi, and the event on the Mount of Transfiguration, Jesus courageously headed toward Jerusalem.

The way Jesus used defeat "to shake the soul and let the glory out" has been a great encouragement through the centuries. Others have emulated him: Lord Kernahan, born without arms and legs, sat in Parliament; Immanuel Kant, anemic of body, wrote great philosophic thoughts; Isaac Watts, battling poverty, invented the steam engine; Beethoven, with his deafness, com-

[2] From "Rabbi Ben Ezra" by Robert Browning.

posed sonatas. You and I too are encouraged by Jesus
to realize that

> *Defeat may serve as well as victory*
> *To shake the soul and let the glory out.*

❧ 25 ☙

BEHOLD THE MAN

BEHOLD THE MAN is an anthology edited by Ralph L.
Woods, in which over four hundred selections from
interpreters as different as Joseph Klausner and Pope
Pius XII, George Santayana and Leo Tolstoy, Virginia
Woolf and Woodrow Wilson, Brigham Young and
Martin Luther express their appreciations of Jesus as
man, God, teacher, redeemer, leader, Messiah, reformer,
and prophet. Poets, theologians, sociologists, statesmen,
playwrights, novelists, and New Testament critics tell
what Jesus meant to them.

"What do you think of Jesus?" is a question every
person must face on his spiritual journey. We face it
today; Jesus' first disciples confronted it (Mk. 8:27–30).
Jesus' ministry in Galilee was disrupted by the enmity of
Herod Antipas, ruler of Galilee; it was disturbed by
Pharisees from Jerusalem who wished to incite Herod's
enmity toward him. Jesus shifted his ministry to the ter-

ritory of Caesarea Philippi, northeast of his Galilean activities, where the more lenient Philip ruled. On the road to Caesarea Philippi Jesus inquired of his disciples, "Who do you say that I am?" It is a question still asked of those who follow him today.

As much as I am moved by the mystery of human existence, I find myself even more awed when I ponder the personality of Jesus. Dean Case calls Jesus the enigma of the centuries to both the saint and the skeptic. He is the most intriguing person to walk in mystery on this little planet. If we today find his way of life and his conception of God so satisfying, is it any wonder that his followers of the first century adorned his name with titles such as "Christ," "Prophet," "Son of God," "Son of Man," "Lord," "the Word," "Saviour"?

Behold the Man! What do we think of Jesus? This we can say: Jesus was a historical person who lived on Palestinian soil, who was crucified under Pontius Pilate in Judea about A.D. 30. Jesus was a Jew, "born of woman" into the family of a carpenter; he had brothers and sisters; he was reared in the Law and the Prophets, the sacred scriptures of the Jews. About ninety-five per cent of Jesus' ethical teachings are found in the Law (Torah) and the rabbinical teachings. Jesus, like every Jew, loved the Torah; it was a lamp unto his feet and a light unto his path. He found the two great commandments, "Love thy God" (Deut. 6:5) and "Love thy neighbor" (Lev. 19:18) in the Torah. His idea of God as a holy, merciful, judging Father, who would give His

104

Kingdom to faithful, repentant people, was found amid the prophets like Amos, Hosea, Isaiah, Jeremiah, and Second Isaiah.

Yet there was something about the person of Jesus which gave a new impression to the ideas which He quoted from the Law and the Prophets. Ethical teachings uttered for centuries by prophets and scribes seemed more distinctly the will of God because Jesus spoke them. As he spoke about God, he seemed to live God's Spirit within his own life. While his first followers were not able to perform fully the teachings he gave to them, they found themselves transformed by his wisdom. The same is true of those who follow him today. Albert Schweitzer, laboring in his medical mission in the Lamberéné region in Africa, has caught the contemporary meaning of Jesus for us:

> He comes to us as One unknown, without a name, as of old, by the lakeside, He came to those men who knew Him not. He speaks to us the same word: "Follow thou me!" and sets us the tasks which He has to fulfil for our time. He commands. And to those who obey Him, whether they be wise or simple, He will reveal Himself in the toils, the conflicts, the sufferings which they shall pass through in His fellowship, and as an ineffable mystery, they shall learn in their own experience.[1] Who He is.

[1] *The Quest of the Historical Jesus* (New York: The Macmillan Co., 1910), p. 401.

Anatole France's short story, "The Procurator of Judaea," portrays Pilate in his old age meeting in Italy a friend, Aelius Lamia, with whom he had shared many experiences in Palestine. After a long conversation about Palestinian events, which Pilate declares "are as vividly present to me as if they had happened yesterday," Lamia mentions having heard of an unusual character named Jesus and asks, "Pontius, do you remember anything about the man?" Pilate hesitatingly answers, "Jesus?. . . . Jesus—of Nazareth? I cannot call him to mind. . . ."

It is one of life's obligations that we "call Jesus to mind." The first disciples were forced to answer the question, "Who do you think that I am?" And so must we. We need to "call Jesus to mind." . . . Behold the man!

❧ 26 ❧

NOTHING MORE DIVINE THAN HIGH
PROPHETIC VISION

Louis Untermeyer once said of Sara Teasdale: "Her later lyrics grew more and more dependent on an inner authority, and less and less upon the clever manipulation of effects." And so has it been with the prophets: they have depended more upon an inner authority than upon the detailed effects of ritual. Said the Lord through Amos the prophet, "Seek me directly as spirit meets

106

Spirit, and not through the ritualistic effects of the sanctuary at Bethel—and ye shall live." As Jesus' friends saw the prophetic authority of God's Spirit in him, they said, "He spoke as one having authority, and not as the scribes (Mt. 7:29)."

The prophets were men of great courage and social passion. They went out with fierce convictions for justice, since they believed that they were God's spokesmen for righteousness. They were not men who made "longtime predictions" about the little details in history; they were primarily persons who spoke "in behalf of" God. Usually lined up with the minorities, they felt themselves God's champions for divine justice in the world. "Was Jesus then only a prophet?" asks Frederick C. Grant. "It is a hard saying, but after all 'prophet' is only one more historical category—and Jesus was unique. In fact, on Jewish lips 'prophet' was the highest possible category, next to God himself. It seems to me that the Incarnation should have taken place through a 'prophet' rather than through one who was only another deluded first-century false Messiah."[1] Jesus seems to feel Himself and His followers a part of the great prophetic tradition, and knows that the task before them is a difficult one: "Men persecuted the prophets who were before you," he told his followers. To His disciples he said, "I have not come to abolish the law and the prophets, but to fulfill them."

T. R. Glover of Cambridge University once said, "The

[1] *Journal of Bible and Religion*, February, 1939.

church as a living thing has always had unsuspected powers of readjustment without losing its life." This readjustment has been due largely to prophetic leadership which has kept the vital religion of the times from becoming a curiosity. As men of tremendous faith in God, the prophets believed that God was able to keep in control of history: as the potter designs his clay, so God designs history. They were not like Voltaire in his earlier days: "God and I nod, but we do not speak." Rather they were "God-intoxicated" men. In line with this idea the Gospel of John in its reflection has Jesus say, "I and the Father are one." On the wall of the humble study of an old German schoolmaster were these words: "Dante, Molière, and Goethe live here"; that teacher's intellectual world was filled with the spirit of these men. So it was with Jesus; his life was so saturated with the Spirit of God, that his followers said, "We who have seen the spirit in the son believe that we have seen the Spirit of the Father."

The prophets were able to practice "alternation" from worship of God to the realm of social reform. They never used worship as a way to escape the world; nor did they believe religion to be merely political-social reform. They desired as God's spokesmen to arouse men to make this world the Kingdom of God. In *The Keys of the Kingdom* by A. J. Cronin, Father Chisholm is bidding good-by to a dying young doctor, who had given his life heroically for the Chinese in an epidemic. Among his last words the doctor says, "I still can't believe in

God." Father Chisholm replies, "Does that matter? He believes in you." Jesus, like the prophets and Father Chisholm, believed that God always believes in those persons who work for social righteousness in the world.

George Eliot sings in one of her poems:

> *The earth yields nothing more Divine*
> *Than high prophetic vision—than the Seer*
> *Who fasting from man's meaner joy beholds*
> *The paths of beauteous order, and constructs*
> *A fairer type, to shame our low content. . . .*[2]

As Joshua and his followers left the wilderness behind and saw the promised land ahead, the Lord said to them, "Sanctify yourselves, for tomorrow God will work wonders among you (Jos. 3:5)." In similar words, Jesus, holding "nothing more Divine than high prophetic vision," speaks to his followers today as he did in the first century. If God is to work wonders on the morrow, it will be through persons of "high prophetic vision."

❧ 27 ❧

GIVE US A VIRILE CHRIST

Give us a virile Christ for these rough days!
You painters, sculptors, show the warrior bold.
And you who turn mere words to gleaming gold,
Too long your lips have sounded in the praise

[2] George Eliot, "Life's Purpose."

Of patience and humility. Our ways
Have parted from the quietude of old;
We need a man of strength with us to hold
The very breach of Death without amaze.
Did He not scourge from temple court the thieves?
And make the arch-fiend's self again to fall?
And blast the fig-tree that was only leaves?
And still the raging tumult of the sea?
Did He not bear the greatest pain of all,
Silent, upon the cross of Calvary?[1]

CERTAIN schools of Christian art have painted Jesus as a weak, otherworldly personality. One of our hymns speaks of him as "gentle Jesus, meek and mild." Such descriptions, however, seem to miss the "virile Christ" of the gospels. Jesus possessed the proper kind of meekness and humility, because his life was centered in God; and he sought the solitude of communion apart from the world. But he primarily shines forth as a man of social passion, with deep courage to face the wrongs of the world. Before the leaders of the Temple and the rulers of Rome he speaks the depth of his convictions.

Victor Hugo analyzes the courage of Jesus in these colorful words:

> To combat Pharisaism, to unmask imposture, to overturn tyrannies, usurpations, prejudices, false-hoods, superstitions—to demolish the temple in order to rebuild it—that is to say, to substitute the true

[1] From "A Virile Christ" by Rex Boundy.

for the false, attack the fierce magistracy, the san-
guinary priesthood; to scourge the money-changers
from the sanctuary; to reclaim the heritage of the
disinherited; to protect the weak, poor, suffering,
and crushed; to combat for the persecuted and
oppressed—such was the war of Jesus Christ!

Only a virile Christ of indomitable courage could battle such evils!

When Jesus in the region of Caesarea Philippi asks his disciples, "Who do men say that I am?" two answers are given: "One of the prophets," and "You are the Christ." Both answers suggest titles of virility. The writings of Isaiah, the prophet, in the Old Testament (Isa. 9, 11) give special stress to a future kingdom of the Israelites to be ushered in by a Messiah, "a prince of peace": "The spirit of the Lord shall rest upon him, the spirit of wisdom and understanding, the spirit of counsel and might, the spirit of knowledge, and of the fear of the Lord. Righteousness shall be the girdle of his loins, and faithfulness the girdle of his reins."

After Isaiah, the Messiah holds a prominent place in national life. He is called King, Judge, Warrior, Conqueror, Servant, Redeemer, Son of Man. He is the one who will bring God's kingdom into history. The hope for such a deliverer came from Israel's confidence that God had a great purpose for her. The Messiah would be of David's line, equipped with God's Spirit; he would bring about a government of justice through truth and love; peace would come for Israel. Certainly none but a virile figure could ever accomplish this end!

While Jesus rejected the use of the sword to accomplish his Kingdom hope (not being a Zealot), he also refused the serene, pacific way of the Essenes who expected the Kingdom to come in small communal groups living quietly apart from the world.

Lewis Browne vividly describes the innate power of Jesus being "the anointed one" (translated "Messiah" in Hebrew, "Christ" in Greek):

> *It is certain that many of those who followed Jesus believed him to be the Messiah. The sight of that ragged young Jew hurrying beneath the hot sun of Galilee, poor, unlearned, yet able to breathe perfect frenzy of hope and cheer into vast throngs of forlorn derelicts, must have been proof indisputable that he was indeed the "Anointed One." There was a wondrous love in his preaching and, coupled with it, an air of certainty, of authority. For five hundred years some Messiah had been awaited, and more than once it had been men of the basest stuff that had been mistaken for Him. Charlatans and madmen, arrant knaves and driveling fools, had time and again been hailed by the hysterical mob as the Awaited One. Is it any wonder, therefore, that an exalted person like this young carpenter, Jesus, should have been hailed likewise?*[2]

[2] *This Believing World* (New York: The Macmillan Co., 1926), p. 267.

At the close of World War I, a group of American chaplains met in Paris before returning to the United States. Said one of them: "We have been trying to show our men that Christianity is a religion to bring them courage and help in time of war. As we go back to a post-war world, we must continue to interpret the Christian faith as that which can bring them aid in facing real life-problems. Unless we do this, we shall fail!" The situation is the same today. We need "a virile Christ for these rough days," and as we see the historical Jesus we realize that we have such a One.

❧ 28 ❧

SHALL WE LOOK FOR ANOTHER?

IN 1929, Harry Elmer Barnes wrote a book entitled, *The Twilight of Christianity*. In this writing he parades the thesis that men like Sherwood Eddy, Jerome Davis, Kirby Page, Frances McConnell, Reinhold Niebuhr, and Harry F. Ward can give us better advice for our age than can Jesus. "Any one of them," he says, "is incomparably superior to Jesus as a guide to both religious and social reconstruction." He further comments: "Dr. Harry Emerson Fosdick is infinitely better able to handle any phase of the problem of personality than was Jesus."

John the Baptist's disciples asked of Jesus, "Are you

he who is to come, or shall we look for another?" Jesus answered them, "Go and tell John what you hear and see: the blind receive their sight and the lame walk, lepers are cleansed and the deaf hear, and the dead are raised up, and the poor have good news preached to them. And blessed is he that takes no offense in me (Mt. 11:3–6)." But Dr. Barnes believes that Jesus and his message belong entirely to a first-century world, certainly not to a twentieth-century, machine-age Western culture. Dr. Barnes represents a type of modern man who says, "We certainly are looking for someone other than Jesus to help solve our contemporary problems."

The modern sophisticated person raises the question: "What can we today learn from a first-century Jew who lived in a remote province of the Roman Empire?" Chester C. McCown has articulate answers for such a query:

> First, men are fundamentally alike in all lands and in all ages that are known to history. The differences are essentially superficial. The second answer is that, in nineteen hundred years, culture has not changed so greatly as moderns like to think, and that Palestine, lying between the east and the west, as the center of the ancient world, was less "provincial" than far-western Rome, or even than unique and learned Athens, for it had a much longer and more varied cultural inheritance. In the third place, the answer is that the Hebrews represent one of

those phenomena which appear again and again in biological and social evolution, different as the two are in many features. A strange and inexplicable combination of circumstances selects certain groups and certain individuals to make them bearers of peculiar values. As a yet undiscovered group of primates developed the human skeleton, as (India) developed the decimal system and (Babylonia) the duodecimal, as (Greece) developed art, science, and philosophy, and (Rome) business, law, and government, so the Jews developed ethics and a spiritual monotheism.[1]

"Are Jesus' insights sufficient for modern living. Or shall we look for another?"

Man wants three things from religion: First, he wants to get along with himself, the *psychological* aspect of religion, in which he hopes to overcome fear, selfishness, resentment, and guilt. Christopher Morley wrote a book several years ago, *The Man Who Made Friends with Himself*. Man wants to "make friends with himself." Do Jesus' insights help man to accomplish this goal?

In the second place, man wants to get along with his fellow men, the *ethical* aspect of religion. Bernard Shaw once said: "That which tears us asunder is irreligious. That which binds us together is religious." Is there any higher way by which men *ought* to live together than by Christian redemptive love?

[1] *The Search for the Real Jesus* (New York: Charles Scribner's Sons, 1940), pp. 301, 302.

Finally, from religion man wants to find his right relationship with God, the *theological* aspect of religion. Jesus taught that men through their repentance and faith could place themselves in touch with God's Spirit. While Jesus saw God distant and awesome, "the Lord of heaven and earth," he also felt that God is as close to man as the breath he breathes. He is one who watches the fall of the sparrow and clothes the lily of the field. Said Jesus: "The Kingdom of God is within." Augustine's words express Jesus' sense of man's need of God: "Our hearts are restless, O God, until they rest in Thee." Jesus showed men how, through their surrender to God, they could quell this restlessness.

A real problem for some today is: "Does Jesus satisfy these three needs of religion, or do we look for another?"

For some like Harry Elmer Barnes, Jesus will remain merely a first-century person with little value for our era. Others will discern Jesus as too far beyond our contemporary reach, as does Oparre in Maxwell Anderson's *The Wingless Victory*, when, before drinking her cup of poison, she cries to her old pagan Malayan gods: "He came too soon, this Christ of peace. Men are not ready yet. Another hundred thousand years they must drink your potion of tears and blood."

There are still others who feel with Paul, that Christ came "in the fulness of time"; that we need not look for another, but must make his insights vital for our century. They venture with C. H. Dodd and say: "The more His Gospel goes out into the wider world, the more clearly does it exhibit its universal character. . . . For our present purpose it is enough to record that after many centuries of historical vicissitude His word is still current, and fertile of new truth."[2]

❦ 29 ❦

MUST HE DIE FOR A DREAM?

Earl Marlatt has written this hymn, frequently sung at conferences of young men and women:

> *"Are ye able," said the Master,*
> *"To be crucified with me?"*
> *"Yea," the sturdy dreamers answered,*
> *"To the death we follow Thee."*
>
> *"Are ye able?" still the Master*
> *Whispers down eternity,*
> *And heroic spirits answer*
> *Now, as then, in Galilee.*[1]

To die for a dream is noble consecration: to carry out such a high ideal is courage at its best. Three times during World War II a missionary friend of mine was brought before Japanese officials and promised release if

[2] *The Authority of the Bible* (New York: Harper and Bros., 1929), pp. 282, 283.
[1] From "The Challenge" by Earl Marlatt.

he would give oath that he would in no way provoke harm against the Japanese nation. Each time he refused to conform to their wishes, largely as a matter of principle rather than a wish to cause destruction of the Japanese people whom he had served for years.

The Christians in Asia Minor during the reign of Emperor Domitian (A.D. 81–96) were promised release from persecution and martyrdom if they would worship Domitian as a god. They refused, for they felt it better to die for the dream of God's Kingdom than to worship one who ruled a temporal kingdom like the Roman Empire. Their loyalties were well calculated, for the Roman Empire crumbled in A.D. 486; God's Kingdom still continues.

Men like Martin Niemoeller refused to worship Adolf Hitler as their saviour; he and others went to concentration camps; many of them were put to death by the Gestapo. "To believe thoroughly in an ideal is to be willing to die for it," expresses the depth of Jesus' concern for the Kingdom of God; and those who have followed him through the centuries have emulated his courage and spirit of consecration.

Jesus was put to death by a plot formed by a few of the Temple gang, some of the Sanhedrin leaders, and the rulers of the Roman government in Palestine. Why Jesus had to die for his dream, however, never has been quite clear in the eyes of theologians; various answers are given. About 1050 the Archbishop of Canterbury, Anselm, developed the "satisfactionary" or "substitutionary" idea of the cross. As the Epistle to the Hebrews stresses Jesus as

the perfect high priest, who offered himself as the perfect sacrifice to God to bring salvation to mankind, so
Anselm wove his view: Mankind has sinned against God;
mankind thus owes God a great debt; but since mankind
is sinful, it cannot pay back this debt to God. Jesus, who
was sinless and owed God nothing, died as a "substitute"
for mankind, and thus "satisfied" divine justice. Thus
salvation of mankind resulted from Jesus' death on the
cross.

About 1100, Abelard, a French theologian, developed
the "moral" theory regarding the death of Jesus. Influ-
enced by the Gospel of Mark, he thus viewed the meaning of Jesus' death: In the gospel story Jesus says to his
disciples: "If any man would come after me, let him
deny himself, take up his cross and follow me." As Jesus
heads toward Jerusalem, leaving the area of Caesarea
Philippi, he shows high courage; he always keeps his ideal
of the Kingdom before him; he retains humility, trust in
God, sympathy for his fellow men, forgiveness toward his
enemies. On the cross before he dies, Jesus cries out in
trust: "Father into thy hands I commit my spirit"; for
his enemies he prays, "Father, forgive them for they
know not what they do." The heroic life of Jesus, carry-
ing his ideals to his death, sets for all of us an example
which "saves" us to our finest Christian personalities.
Because Jesus dies for his dream of the Kingdom, we are
constrained to emulate him. "There is that strange man
upon his cross who draws me back again and again," said
George Tyrrell in his tragic experience of excommunica-

tion from his church. So are the rest of us attracted to "that strange man upon his cross"; in being enamored by the life of Jesus, we are saved into living for God's Kingdom.

Must he die for a dream? Both Jesus and Alexander the Great were thirty-three when they died. Each had a dream of world conquest: Alexander desired Greece to rule the world; Jesus wished God's reign to come on earth. Alexander died after a drunken orgy; his empire fell into the hands of the Romans two hundred years later. Jesus died because of his labor for God's Kingdom; the dream he possessed nineteen hundred years ago is still the hope of the world!

George Eliot once said that the early Christians were cowards because they did not die with Jesus. Most of us today are not asked to die for Jesus' dream of the Kingdom; but we are asked to live for it!

〰 30 〰

THEY SAW JESUS ONLY

IN 1944, I received an invitation to lecture at an inter-denominational conference of ministers in one of our American cities. A sentence in the letter caught my eye: "In this time of confusion we want to make a careful study of Jesus in the light of modern scholarship to see what Jesus has to say to our contemporary problems." The ministers wanted through a week of lectures and discussions to "see Jesus only." As Christian ministers they had accepted Jesus as "the way, the truth, and the life"; but in our complex civilization, they wanted to ponder more deeply what their confession about Jesus meant. The early Christians meditated on the meaning of Jesus as "the Christ." To them the transfiguration event (Mk. 9:2–8), following Peter's confession, "Thou art the Christ," meant that Jesus as the Christ is the incarnation of the Divine Spirit. He is an earthly figure, human in his qualities; but he is also one who reflects the Spirit of God. As a later New Testament writer said: "The Word became flesh and dwelt among us, full of grace and truth; we have beheld his glory, glory as of the only Son from the Father (Jn. 1:14)."

The transfiguration story expresses in poetry and theology what Jesus said in words to his disciples: "I have not come to abolish the law and the prophets; I have come not to abolish them but to fulfill them." Moses was the Father of the Law, Elijah was the Father of Prophecy. Each had been transfigured: Elijah was caught in a whirlwind and carried up to God. "Moses went up into the mount, and a cloud covered the mount. And the glory of the Lord abode upon Mount Sinai, and the cloud covered it six days." The Mount of Transfiguration expresses the view of the early Christians: "Jesus answers the hopes of both the law and the prophets. He is the answer to our centuries-long hope. Jesus as the interpreter of God's will is all we now need." Hence, after his transfiguration, "they saw Jesus only."

Today also men see Jesus only! But they see him through the eyes of modern interpreters: Rudolf Bultmann sees "Jesus only" as "the Word" of recent German theology; for him Jesus seems an interpreter of twentieth-century European theology. Dmitri Merejkowski sees "Jesus only" as one who is the center of Russian mysticism; one who adds something mysterious to life which makes it richly different. Albert Schweitzer sees "Jesus only" as the unseen companion in Africa and other parts of the world for those who follow him; though in the first century Schweitzer viewed him as one who was to return as the Son of Man upon the clouds shortly after his death. Some look upon "Jesus only" as what Robert Keable calls "the literary Jesus"; different groups—socialist, prohibitionist, pacifist, communist, militarist—find Jesus as their guide and norm. John Baillie looks upon "Jesus only" as the symbol of redeeming, suffering love. A mystic like the late Charles Andrews sees "Jesus only" as the living comrade, an "eternal contemporary" who invisibly walks with his followers. Some see "Jesus only" as the equivalent for God: "I find that Jesus gives me everything for which I desire in God."

Those who today see "Jesus only" perceive him spiritually. They use his insights into religion for their personal and social living, to "see" if his way of life "works." Jesus called some of the Pharisees in his day, who saw religion mainly as making promises at the altar and going through the details of ritual, "blind guides"; the "Shekinah" (the glorious presence of God) would never shine upon them.

Those today who see "Jesus only" with spiritual eyes find the Christian religion something which lifts them to mountaintops of spiritual experience.

One of Rudyard Kipling's great novels is *The Light that Failed.* It is the story of an artist Dick Heldar, who goes into the Sudan to make illustrations. He becomes successful, and falls in love with a shallow, selfish artist named Maisie. Dick gradually goes blind, due to an eye injury received in the Sudan, but he continues to work on his great masterpiece, "Melancholia." Maisie, realizing that blindness soon will come upon Dick, deserts him. *The Light that Failed* is a story of the world; but not the story of the New Testament Jesus, as "the true light that enlightens every man coming into the world," never fails those who see him only.

A man blind for years recently recovered his sight. His first words were: "Oh! Lord how wondrous and how glorious are all thy works!" And so is the exclamation of many who see "Jesus only" in their daily living.

Sadhu Singh expresses the change in his life after he saw "Jesus only." "Without Christ I was like a fish out of water, or like a bird in the water. With Christ I am in the ocean of love, and while in the world, am in heaven. For all this, to Him be praise and glory and thanksgiving forever."[1]

[1] *With and Without Christ* (London: Cassell and Co., 1929), p. 129.

❧ 31 ❧

WHAT MAKES A MAN GREAT?

A FEW years ago Billy Rose, in his newspaper column, told of a meeting, in 1923, at the Edgewater Beach Hotel in Chicago, of seven of the most powerful financial leaders in the world. These seven men controlled more wealth than was in the United States Treasury: Arthur Cutten, greatest wheat speculator in the world; Richard Whitney, president of the New York Wheat Exchange; Albert Fall, member of the President's Cabinet; Jesse Livermore, the leading "bear" on Wall Street; Leon Fraser, president of the Bank of International Settlement; Ivar Krueger, head of the world's greatest monopoly; Charles Schwab, president of the largest independent steel company in the world. Certainly men of tremendous power, "great" in the eyes of the business world! But where were they in 1948, twenty-five years later? Cutten died abroad, insolvent; Schwab lived on borrowed money the last five years of his life, and died penniless; Fraser, Livermore, and Krueger committed suicide; Whitney spent a period of time in prison at Sing Sing; Fall was released from a prison sentence that he might die at home.

As I read the story of these men, I asked myself: "What makes a man great?" And then I remembered

124

Jesus' words, "What does it profit a man, if he gain the
whole world, yet lose his own soul? (Mk. 8:36)"

Greatness and power are often closely associated. James
and John, sons of Zebedee, wanted the chief seats in the
kingdom, "one at your right hand and one at your left,
in your glory." Jesus' reply to them was that he came
"not to be served but to serve." At another time Jesus'
disciples were discussing the question: "Who is the greatest?" He told them: "If any man would be first, he must
be last of all and servant of all. . . . He who humbles himself will be exalted. . . . Greater love hath no man than
this, that a man lay down his life for his friends." To
hear Jesus' words is to realize that his idea of what makes
a man great is not in accordance with that of the average
man's definition.

"The greatest use of life is to spend it for something
that outlasts it," said William James. Jesus agreed with
this statement. He said: "He who loses his life for my
sake and the gospel's will save it." Jesus was right! A
study of history shows many of our major civilizations
have gone the way of destruction, while the kingdom of
God has continued as a reality. One day a friend said to
the great Russian Turgenev, "The secret of living is to
put yourself in second place." To which Turgenev replied, "No. The secret of living is to know what to put
in first place!" The goal of greatness, in which one allows
himself to be absorbed in something worth while, is the
secret of a life purpose. Jesus suggested God's Kingdom
as this goal.

In the nineteenth century, Friedrich Nietzsche looked upon Christianity as a religion only for soft, aenemic persons; it appealed to weak individuals. To replace Christianity he wove the concept of the "superman" and the "super-race" into which people of strength should throw themselves. At the close of World War I an Austrian paper hanger, Adolf Hitler, enticed by this concept of greatness, was able to win Germany to accept his totalitarian view. He convinced the German nation that it was made up of a super-race of Nordic people which ought to control the world through employment of military power. A nation which had given to the world such persons as Bach and Beethoven, Kant and Schleiermacher, Dürer and Wagner, Luther and Harnack was deceived into believing that the way out of its dilemma was through the philosophy of the "superman" and the "super-race." Germany went the "way of all flesh," much to the sorrow of many of her friends throughout the world, who knew that nation had been misled by her leaders as to what makes a nation—or a man—great.

Hitler's catastrophe made many people realize that the way to greatness lies not through power, but through loyalty to God and service to mankind. "After Hitler came to power," writes Emil Brunner, "it suddenly dawned on a great many people who theretofore had not bothered at all about Christianity that the stake in the fight against Hitler was nothing less than the foundations of our life, of our whole civilization."

How much safer we would feel today if atomic power

were in the hands of humble, yet great, men like St. Francis of Assisi, Gandhi, Kagawa, George Fox, Phillips Brooks—for these men viewed greatness through the pattern of service to mankind. Those who see greatness in terms of Christians working in partnership with God for the betterment of mankind are never dismayed by evil days. Instead of complaining, "Look what the world has come to," they cry out, "Look what has come to the world"; and with greatness defined in terms of service, they go out and labor with God for His Kingdom on earth.

❧ 32 ☙

HOW OFTEN SHOULD ONE FORGIVE?

THE NOVEL by Johan Bojer, *The Great Hunger*, tells the story of Peer Holm. It is the portrait of a man in quest of his soul, "a composite of Prometheus, Job, and St. Francis. Like Prometheus he must suffer for his virtue, like Job he must face his trials with meekness and unswerving faith, like St. Francis he must return good for evil, bread for stones." Reared in poverty, by great endeavor he becomes educated as an engineer; culture, wealth, and power follow; yet Peer Holm is dissatisfied, for he has not found the meaning of life. Then come reversals; he loses all, and suffers disillusionment. He finally realizes what is missing in his quest: Christian

Love. He faces another crisis when his lovely child is killed by the mad dog of a feuding neighbor who lives on the adjoining farm. But Peer Holm does not seek revenge. Out of his poverty, though it means that he and his family will go without food, he secretly takes seed to his neighbor's field for the spring sowing. "I went out and sowed the corn in my enemy's field, that God might exist." Through Christian forgiveness and love, Peer Holm found God.

"How often should a man forgive a person who wrongs him?" is the gist of the question Peter asks Jesus. "Not seven times, but seventy times seven (Mt. 18:21, 22)," is Jesus' reply. Forgiveness is an attitude rather than a number of acts; "seventy times seven" in Oriental metaphor means "always." Jesus implies that God, the most wronged of all, eternally forgives and without reservation. If man is to be perfect as his heavenly Father is perfect, man cannot forgive less. Forgiveness cannot be a one-sided affair; if we cannot forgive men who injure us, then God is not able to forgive us. "Atonement" from God means "at-one-ment" with our fellow men; we must have a single spirit, not a double spirit. "If you forgive men their trespasses, your heavenly Father also will forgive you; but if you do not forgive men their trespasses, neither will your Father forgive your trespasses."

Twenty years ago I heard T. Z. Koo of China speak at an international Christian meeting in Cleveland, Ohio. In his address he said that the one event in Jesus' life which finally attracted him from Confucianism to Christianity was Jesus' attitude on the cross toward his malefactors. "To hear a man offer forgiveness toward those who had done their worst, who had crucified him, won me to the Christian faith." The one who had said, "Forgive seventy times seven," meant it; for on the cross he prayed for his enemies: "Father, forgive them for they know not what they do." Jesus was a living example of his own teaching about forgiveness.

The person who forgives one who wrongs him brings help to an enemy; he also "destroys" his enemy by forgiving him. But to forgive an enemy brings even more value to the "forgiver." Trying to get even with a person is one of the easiest ways to wreck one's health. An article in *Life* magazine said, "The chief personality characteristic of persons with hypertension (high blood pressure) is resentment. When resentment is chronic, hypertension and heart trouble follow." To "forgive seventy times seven" is not only good religion; it is excellent medicine. Dr. Irving Fisher, the economist, found that one half of five thousand business failures were traceable to personality failures; back of these personality failures were men and women whose lives were eaten by hatred and fear. Energy in their lives, released by forgiveness and warmth toward their fellow men, in many instances could have spelled success. Hatred and revenge release toxic poisons in the blood stream. The American Medical Association has approved figures showing that fifty per cent of man's illness is caused by wrong mental-spiritual attitudes.

When hatred and revenge are replaced by forgiveness and sympathy, a right step toward health is taken.

We can never expect nations to forgive one another unless people within those nations forgive each other. The starting place for world peace is in individuals finding peace with one another. In each person Christian forgiveness is basic:

> Unless within my heart I hold
> Abiding peace,
> No league of nations can succeed,
> Nor will strife cease.
>
> If I myself see every fault
> In kin and friend,
> The world may never see the day
> When war will end.[1]

How often should a man forgive? After Peer Holm sowed the corn in his enemy's field, he exclaimed, "Ah! if you had known that moment! It was as if the air about me grew alive with voices!"

❧ 33 ❧

WHO IS MY NEIGHBOR?

JESUS defined a religious person as one who showed mercy toward his neighbor in need; anyone in want

[1] Copyright 1942 by The Curtis Publishing Company.

is a neighbor (Lk. 10:25–37). The Christian today sees
the whole world as a locality where he must play the
"Good Samaritan." For the narrow ritualistic Jew, a
Samaritan was outside the fold of God's salvation because as a Jew he had intermarried with a Gentile; for
Jesus, a Samaritan was within the pale of God's Kingdom
if he showed redemptive love toward a person in need.
A modern Japanese Christian, catching the spirit of universalism as shown in Jesus, held this as his philosophy:

> *I for Japan,*
> *Japan for the world,*
> *The world for Jesus,*
> *All for God.*

While Jesus was first of all concerned with the salvation
of his own countrymen—"the lost sheep of the house of
Israel"—he was further desirous of God's Kingdom mov-
ing out to reach all humanity.

Who is my neighbor? Two experiences come to my
memory: (1) A few years ago on a college campus, I
heard five men speak on the theme, "What religion
means to me." The speakers were a Roman Catholic
bishop, a Jewish rabbi, a minister of a Community
Church, a theological professor, a minister of a metropolitan Methodist Church. While each person had a different external authority behind his religious views, each
of them wanted the same things from religion: (a) each
wanted to get along with himself, the psychological phase
of religion; (b) each wanted to live via love in right

relationships with his fellow men, the *ethical* phase of religion; (c) each wanted to live close to God, the *theological* phase of religion. These five were "neighbors" in wanting the same basic aids from religion.

Rabbi Louis Finkelstein speaks for Judaism regarding the world as a "neighborhood":

> The "One World" which will emerge need not be a single empire or commonwealth or church or civilization, but *an association of men entirely free and independent, and yet mutually loving; an association based on the close ties* and informality of *brotherhood,* rather than on the bonds of formal organization; "an association to do the will of God with a perfect heart."[1]

Ross Sanderson, a Protestant, speaks in similar words:

> Once again Christianity faces a great historic opportunity, this time with far larger hope of success (than in the fifteenth century) by reason of the gains achieved during four Protestant centuries. . . . We move toward a time when *the entire church will function ecumenically at all levels,* through the cooperative churchmanship of all communions.[2]

Father John LaFarge of the Roman Catholic Church says:

[1] Willard L. Sperry (editor), *Religion in the Post-War World* (Harvard University Press, 1945), p. 94.
[2] *Christendom,* IX, 1944.

The most efficacious attempts that will ever be made toward reconciliation between the different Christian bodies will chiefly occur on the personal rather than on the formally ecclesiastical scale. It is in lowly living, in humble approach to God, in prayer and penance and good works that the foundation may be laid for common understanding. . . . As the world grows closer to God, as the world is humbled, as the world is purified, it will come to a deeper knowledge and an eventual understanding of that mystery of unity and diversity which is his own life and which is the expression, the bond, of his own personal relation with the Saviour himself.[3]

(2) In 1928, my wife and I spent Christmas in Germany. After we had gone on Christmas eve to a beautiful church service, we returned to our pension. Amid the festivities about the white Christmas tree, my German friend, Herr Karl Falke, spoke to our small group of five persons on "Liebe und Friede" (love and peace). After his talk, I said to him, "Isn't it peculiar, Karl, that a little over ten years ago you and I were supposed to be enemies, you in the German army, I in the American army? And yet tonight you speak to me about 'love and peace.' "

When Jews, Roman Catholics, and Protestants look at each other with prophetic-Christian eyes, they realize that each is the other's neighbor. When people of different countries view one another through eyes of Christian

[3] *Ibid.*, p. 5.

love, they know that they are neighbors in God's Great Commonwealth. When Jesus saw a Samaritan showing mercy toward an injured man, he told his story about, "Who is my neighbor?" This simple story is today the foundation for world brotherhood.

A great Quaker poet, John Greenleaf Whittier, catching Jesus' definition of a neighbor, wrote these words:

O brother man, fold to thy heart thy brother;
Where thy pity dwells, the peace of God is there;
To worship rightly is to love each other,
Each smile a hymn, each kindly deed a prayer.

Follow with reverent steps the great example
Of Him whose holy work was doing good;
So shall the wide earth seem our Father's temple,
Each loving life a psalm of gratitude.

❧ 3 4 ☙

LIFE IS LENT TO BE SPENT

EVERYDAY as well as on the first Palm Sunday, life is lent to be spent. Jesus once said to his disciples: "If any man would come after me, let him deny himself and take up his cross and follow me. Whoever would save his life will lose it." Strange words, yet wise words, for Jesus' disciples then as now!

On the first Palm Sunday (Mk. 11:1–11) Jesus' friends

134

are taking these words seriously; they are devoted to the one whom they are following. We see them now as they move toward Jerusalem. At Jericho some had cut palm branches (Jn. 12:13) [usually carried by crowds at the Feast of Tabernacles]. Now they are throwing them as symbols of victory along Jesus' pathway as he rides an ass, a beast of burden. Do they understand the nature of his triumph? That he will receive a cross and not a crown? Do they understand why he rides an ass? Possibly Jesus is tired after the long climb from Jericho. Or perhaps he believes himself to be a messenger of peace. Only Jesus himself knows.

As Jesus' followers come over the Mount of Olives, they see Jerusalem and the Temple on the hill. In their midst rides the prophet of Galilee, whose preaching about God's Kingdom has filled them with eager expectation. As they view their palms, their enthusiasm breaks into shouts of praise: "Hosanna—O God, help us now. Blessed is he who comes in the name of the Lord!" Before the Temple gates the crowd breaks forth in singing:

Lift up your heads, O ye gates,
And be ye lifted up, ye ancient doors,
That the King of glory may come in!

We cannot miss the joy of Jesus' followers. How they love the Temple, where God is worshiped at the great feasts! Jesus believes that he has the secret of peace for Jerusalem. But the Temple officials oppose his message. Jesus believes that the spiritual blindness and the rebellious attitude of Judaism's leaders will lead to the doom of Jerusalem. He sees the end toward which things are tending in Judea. His message to Israel is a last intervention from the God of peace, but the Temple officials refuse to hear it. The mind of Jesus is weighted not so much with his own sorrow as with the city's doom. "When he drew nigh he saw the city, and wept over it . . ." for he foresaw its destruction.

Before returning to Bethany at evening, Jesus takes a glance at the Temple. Possibly he is contemplating "the morrow" when he will cleanse the Temple of its commercial evils and its bad practices. The Temple system has become corrupt like a fig tree no longer able to bring forth spiritual fruit to its people because it has lost its spiritual rootage. As Jesus walks slowly from the Temple to Bethany, does he see the shadow of a wooden cross before him? Jesus' life is lent to be spent to do the will of God. The ascent to Golgotha is not many hours away. . . .

We are living in the twentieth century. Jesus' teachings still speak to man's unchanging spiritual needs. Life is still lent to be spent if we are to be followers of Jesus. Many people today are unhappy and frustrated; they have no peace; they rush about weary and perplexed; they never succeed in forgetting themselves. Many with nothing wrong go to doctors for treatment. There are many in our hospitals and asylums whose selfishness will not let them spend themselves in something bigger than self-interest. What inner torment many might avoid if they would listen to Jesus' words: "He that is greatest among you shall be your servant/ . . . Let him take up his cross and follow me . . . whoever would save his life would lose it."

In Edna Ferber's novel, *So Big,* a young woman teacher is having trouble in getting along with herself, and wishes to run away from the problems of living. An old, mature Dutch housewife says to her, "You can't run away from life, missy; you can't run away far enough." She is right: we cannot escape from life. Holy Week demands that we face life, for God has lent us our lives to be spent in aiding Him to bring His Kingdom on earth!

ᘒ 35 ᘔ

HE PREACHED AS NEVER SURE TO PREACH AGAIN

As Jesus retired to Bethany on the evening of Palm Sunday, his mind could not erase what he had seen in the Court of the Gentiles in the Temple. Tables had been set up for changing copper coins into silver-alloy coins minted at Tyre, used to pay the one-half shekel (32¢) head tax on each male Israelite; the proceeds were to support the Temple. These tables were usually placed in the Temple three weeks before the Passover and taken down after seven days of moneychanging.

Jesus was not criticising the head tax; he was objecting to placing the tables in the Court of the Gentiles because this encumbered the area for Gentile worship. He was protesting that much of the profits from the money-changing was bulging the pockets of bankers, business-men, and the Temple cliques instead of beautifying the Temple.

Booths for selling birds and animals were crowding other sections of the Court of the Gentiles. This graft was controlled by the Saducean priestly families of Boethus and Annas, whom the people hated for their profiteering. The rabbis of Jesus' time criticised these priestly grafters: "Away from here, you sons of Eli, who have dishonored the Temple of the Lord!" The Temple, built as a place in which men could worship God, had become "a den of robbers," a sinful spot where selfish priests and a lay crowd stuffed their pockets.

Jesus has decided that he will strike at the evils in the Temple system which are holding back the coming of God's Kingdom. Jesus is to preach, though never sure to preach again! As he cleanses the Temple (Mk. 11:15–17) we see the zealous prophet of social righteousness stand-ing out against a rotting priestly caste. The grandeur of his courage and righteous wrath are clearly contrasted with the fouling of the Temple. This act is to hasten his death on the cross, because it increases the rising hatred toward him. The Temple bosses know that unless they destroy Jesus, whom the multitudes hear gladly, the Tem-ple system will be destroyed. The Temple clique has great power; within a few days it will convince the Roman rulers that Jesus is worthy of crucifixion. Jesus as a prophet is hitting at the evils of organized priestly religion.

We need both the prophet and the priest in religion. Without the priest we would not have church organization, hymns, creeds, ritual, ceremony, a Bible. Priestly religion by itself faces the danger of becoming static, an escape for those who make a business out of religion. The prophet is on the side of progress. His voice sometimes is too far ahead of the people. The prophet needs the priest to catch the newness of his message and to make it a part of the organized faith, so that such religion will remain an adventure and not an empty show. The priest and the prophet work together.

Jesus is not against priestly religion. He goes to the great festivals at Jerusalem, he pays the half-shekel tax, he wears tassels on his tunic, perhaps he wears the phylactery (prayerbox) on his forearm or forehead. Nor is Jesus against the Jewish Law: he loves the Law; it is a lamp unto his feet and a light unto his path; in it he finds the two great commandments, "Love thy God" and "Love thy neighbor." Jesus, however, is against allowing ceremonial rites of the Temple to become a barrier instead of an aid to the coming of God's Kingdom. Cleansing the Temple of its wrongs would initiate Jesus' dramatic effort to bring God's Kingdom on earth. But it is too late to change the Temple system. Jesus is not a religious reformer who will put a new patch on the timeworn robe of the system. He knows that the old wineskins of the Temple system will not hold the living wine of his prophetic teachings. The Temple crowd and their followers will be the last to receive the Kingdom; his friends who are following his way will be the first.

The Temple crowd wonder where Jesus gets the authority for his message. Jesus' authority comes directly from God. Religion for Jesus is a "feeling of absolute dependence on God"; it is an experience which supports him in this tragic hour, not something which he must support by a rotting Temple system. Because he is doing God's will, and knows from whom his authority comes,

> He preached as never sure to preach again,
> And as a dying man to dying men.[1]

The cross is drawing closer!

⟨⟨ 36 ⟩⟩

HE BELIEVED ENOUGH TO BE GREAT

LOYALTY to both God and the Roman government was a burning issue in Jesus' day. In A.D. 6 the Roman governors imposed a head tax of a silver denarius (16¢) on each male Israelite, to be paid by a coin which bore the name or image of the Roman emperor. When a census was taken among the Jews to determine those who should pay, a revolt arose among the Zealots, who felt that to pay this tax to Rome was betraying God as "King."

The popularity of Jesus at the Passover disturbed the Temple clique. If they could obtain from him some state-

[1] Richard Baxter, "A Preacher's Urgency."

ment which would make him show treason toward Rome, they could rid themselves of him by turning him over to the Roman officials. In asking Jesus about paying the head tax to Caesar they hoped to snare him. However, when he replied, "Pay to Caesar that which belongs to Caesar, and to God that which belongs to God (Mk. 12:17)," he was in harmony with the rabbis of his time who were saying, "Pray for the peace of the Roman kingdom." Like the Pharisees, Jesus accepted the power of Rome until God should give His deliverance to His faithful followers. The Zealots, who urged that taxes paid to Rome showed disloyalty to God, were the only religious party whom Jesus offended.

The Pharisees and the Sadducees represented the important parties of Judaism. Both groups held membership in the supreme court of Judaism, the Sanhedrin, but their religious views differed. The Pharisees, with the rabbis, believed in the resurrection of the dead. The Sadducees believed that man's soul remained in Sheol (realm of the dead), since the Law did not teach the idea of the resurrection. In trying to trap Jesus in his belief about the resurrection, the Sadducees asked him about a woman who had married seven husbands: "Whose wife will she be on the resurrection day? (Mk. 12:18–27)" Jesus replied, "The Law, which you revere, teaches that God is the God of the living; Abraham, Isaac, and Jacob are living now with Him. Furthermore, earthly life is one thing; heavenly life is another experience."

In his belief about the resurrection, Jesus shared the

views of the Pharisees and of the rabbis, who believed that "the world to come is not like this world. In the world to come there is no eating and drinking, no begetting of children, no bargaining, no jealousy and hatred and strife."

An exciting question among the rabbis in Jesus' day was: "Which is the greatest commandment? (Mk. 12: 28–34)" Some followed Rabbi Hillel: "What is hateful to thyself, do not to thy neighbor; this is the whole law, the rest is commentary." Some said, "To love thy God is the greatest commandment," which was part of the Jewish *Shema* (credo), repeated twice daily by male Jews. Other rabbis felt that the statement of Habakkuk, the prophet, was the highest utterance: "The righteous man lives by his faithfulness." Jesus' reply regarding the greatest commandment accorded with the best of rabbinical thought: "Thou shalt love the Lord thy God with all thy heart, and with all thy soul, and with all thy mind (Deut. 6:5)"; and "Thou shalt love thy neighbor as thyself (Lev. 19:18)." Jesus was identified as a person in harmony with the soundest teachings of Judaism. It thus cannot be a religious heresy charge upon which Jesus will be tried before the Sanhedrin.

It was once said of Marcus Aurelius, philosopher and Roman emperor: "He did not believe enough to be great." This cannot be said of Jesus. He believed in proper loyalty to the state, in supreme loyalty to God; he believed in the resurrection of the dead; he believed that love of God and neighbor are basic in God's plan for the

142

Kingdom. Had the Temple clique, the gang from the Sanhedrin, and the Zealots shared the religious views of Jesus and rabbinic Judaism, the story of Jerusalem and the Temple might have turned out differently. In A.D. 66 the Zealots took up the sword against Rome; by 70 the Temple was destroyed and Jerusalem was demolished. Jesus believed that he held the secret which would save Jerusalem from her plight. If only her leaders would believe in him and his message, she could be saved from her shallow religious practices and her nationalistic dreams. "O Jerusalem, Jerusalem!" Jesus cried in agony (Mt. 23: 37). . . .

Now we live in our century. . . . We are called a "cutflower civilization" with no deep religious roots. . . . Are we believing too little about God, about the relation of religion to the state, about love to neighbors, about the significance of Jesus, about life after death? During Holy Week, a time to dedicate ourselves to beliefs which can make us great, let this be the heart of our "credo":

> *This is our faith tremendous,*
> *Our wild hope, who shall scorn,*
> *That in the name of Jesus*
> *The world shall be reborn.*[2]

The Temple clique and the Roman rulers in Palestine did not believe enough to be great! Jesus did! And so must we, if Western culture is to be saved!

[2] Vachel Lindsay, "Foreign Missions in Battle Array" from *Collected Poems*. Copyright 1925 by The Macmillan Company. Reprinted by permission of the publishers.

❦ 37 ❦

BY ALL MEANS USE SOME TIME
TO BE ALONE

WEDNESDAY and Friday became fast days in sections of the early church: Friday was so observed because it was the day of the crucifixion; Wednesday, on account of Judas' betrayal of Jesus. During Jesus' "last week" his public activities have been exhausting. He now feels the necessity of retiring to Bethany to renew his strength and poise for the tragic events which lie ahead. He knows the value of the words:

> By all means use some time to be alone;
> Salute thyself; see what thy soul doth wear;
> Dare to look into thy chest, for 'tis thy own.[1]

On this day of retirement in Bethany two things happen (Mk. 14:3–11): (1) the anointment of Jesus; (2) the betrayal by Judas Iscariot. Anointment of a person with olive and vegetable oils or perfumes was not unusual in Palestine. The dry climate necessitated the use of oils for the body. At fashionable dinners, hosts anointed the heads and beards, and sometimes the feet, of guests as a mark of hospitality. Jesus' anointment with fragrant oil in this Bethany home was an Oriental custom, yet a bit unusual in a home without wealth. It was thus not out

[1] George Herbert, "The Church Porch."

144

of place for guests to upbraid the woman for pouring costly perfume so lavishly over Jesus' head.

Was the pouring of the perfume on Jesus in this event an ordinary act of hospitality? Or did it mean that among Jesus' friends he was accepting himself as "the anointed one"? (The term "Messiah" from the Hebrew, and the title "Christ" from the Greek, mean "the anointed one.") The gospel story indicates that it was more than a mark of hospitality, that it was a devout act in which Jesus accepted himself as God's Messiah.

Perhaps Jesus at this time reflected upon Psalm 23 where the psalmist, pressed on all sides by his foes, accepted God's gracious hospitality at a festive banquet:

> *Thou preparest a table before me*
> *In the presence of mine enemies;*
> *Thou anointest my head with oil.*
> *My cup runneth over.*
> *Surely goodness and mercy shall follow me*
> *All the days of my life;*
> *And I will dwell in the house of the Lord*
> *Forever . . . and ever*

The anointment of Jesus serves as a prologue to the passion drama which soon follows. One of Jesus' followers now goes to the chief priests to tell them what has happened. So we come to the betrayal. We wonder just why Judas betrayed Jesus. Was Judas merely a selfish person who wanted thirty pieces of silver ($15)? Could he have theorized that Jesus was too slow in making himself Messiah, and that betrayal would force his program to a dramatic finish? Did Judas, as a Judean, feel Jesus a dangerous figure who would soon cause riots at the Passover? Was Judas convinced that Jesus was wrong in taking the role of "the anointed one"? The early church did not clearly understand Judas' motives, nor can we. Care is needed in judgment of Judas: "Let him that is without sin among you cast the first stone." Only God and Judas at this time know the full motive for Judas' betrayal.

Jesus is not in quiet retirement to escape the problems of Holy Week. He knows how to practice "alternation" between worship and social activity. He is finding in his closeness with his Father a power and a wisdom which will give him courage and ability to carry his mission before his enemies and on to Golgotha. He knows how "to be in the world but not of it."

Americans are sometimes more concerned with the fruits than the roots of worship. If we are to find the direction toward which our religious activities should be focused, we need to "use some time to be alone." Religion is defined as "what one does with one's solitude." A person who never takes time to be alone will never be deeply religious. Thomas More, advisor to Henry VIII, retired each Friday to his estate in Chelsea to be alone with God. George Washington Carver spent several hours each morning alone with God before beginning his labors in his chemical laboratory. Man cannot live his best without the creative use of solitude.

The gospel portrait shows Jesus continuously "alternating" from retirement in worship to ethical activity among his fellow men. From the temptation scene he turned to his Galilean ministry; from the transfiguration scene he shifted to the "last week" at Jerusalem; from this day of retirement, he will soon face his accusers with his gospel of salvation. If we are to be his disciples, can we do less than to follow his pattern of living?

By all means use some time to be alone. . . .

❧ 38 ❧

AFRAID TO DIE?

T HE GREAT event of the Old Testament is the crossing of the Red Sea. Without this deliverance from Egypt, Judaism never would have been. Each year on 15 Nisan (March–April), at the Passover, the Jews celebrate their freedom from Egypt. Near the time of this festival Jesus, with his disciples, is making his last visit at Jerusalem.

In preparation for the Passover, lambs were selected on the Sabbath preceding the feast. On the eve of 13 Nisan, all leaven was searched for with candlelight by the family head, then burned or thrown to the winds on the following day. All except necessary work stopped by noon of 14 Nisan. On the evening of 15 Nisan, from ten to twenty ate a lamb between eight days and one year old, sacrificially killed by the priest.

The Passover meal consisted of bitter herbs, unleavened cakes, the Passover lamb, the *hagigah* (free-will festal offering), and the *haroseth* (fruits, dates, raisins, mixed with vinegar). All these remind the participants of the hardships, bitterness, and sufferings of their forefathers in Egypt, in their struggle for freedom, and in their wilderness wanderings.

At the Passover meal four cups of wine were drunk: With the first cup the head of the house offered the blessing; ceremonial handwashing with a prayer came next, followed by everyone eating of the bitter herbs in the *haroseth.* As the second cup of wine was drunk, the family head explained the feast; the third cup of wine was followed by grace after meals; with the fourth cup of wine the *Hallel* (Psalms 113–118) was sung.

The Passover, however, was not the meal eaten by Jesus and his disciples shortly before his death: They ate *artos* (ordinary bread) and not *azuma* (Passover bread); Jesus, according to the Gospel of John, was crucified on the day the priests prepared the Passover lambs. The "last supper" eaten by Jesus and his circle of friends was an ordinary meal, which has become "The Lord's Supper" in Christian memories. As the group at this meal reclined on couches around the table, Jesus, knowing that the end was near, enacted a parable (Mk. 14:22–25). In giving pieces of broken bread to his friends, he foresaw that his own body would be thus broken by death. In drinking of the cup of wine with his disciples— the cup of benediction—he added his faith that their separation was to be brief, for soon God would reunite them when He would give them His Kingdom. The meal closed with a hymn.

After the hymn was sung, Jesus retired to the Mount of Olives, and then to Gethsemane where he prayed in agony, believing he would soon be snared by his enemies: "Not what I will, but what thou wilt." This prayer portrays the strange mixture of anguish and trust in Jesus' soul; it pictures the soul of every man who faces tragic circumstances, yet aware that

> *Behind the dim unknown*
> *Standeth God within the shadow,*
> *Keeping watch above His own.*[1]

Jesus might have hidden that night from his enemies and escaped into Galilee. But Jesus was not like that. In the Gethsemane struggle we observe one of the greatest prayer scenes in all religious history; it shows deep religious triumph; Jesus is not afraid to die. It is the story of you and me at our best as religious creatures.

When Christians celebrate the "last supper" it is called Holy Communion, the Eucharist, the Mass, the Lord's Supper. Terms like "transubstantiation," "consubstantiation," "real presence," "symbols of remembrance," "channels of grace" are used to interpret the meaning of the bread and the wine. Whatever our religious faith, as we partake of the mysteries of this festival, we share a common hope that we become "transubstantiated" (have a

[1] From "The Present Crisis" by James Russell Lowell.

real change) from our sinful and frail selves into divine, Christlike persons. As we come from the table of Our Lord may we share the courage, framed in vivid words by a soldier on the battlefield before his death:

> Well, I have to go now, God; good by
> Strange, since I met you,
> I'm not afraid to die.

The confidence in such prayers prepares us for the Good Friday events which sooner or later come to all of us.

·❦· 39 ·❦·

I'VE PUT OUT MY HAND AND TOUCHED THE FACE OF GOD

"THERE comes a midnight hour when all men must unmask." With reflection upon these words every person contemplates the mystery of his own death. Yet there is even more mystery about the death of Jesus. Why, we ask, did Jesus need to die?

The trial of Jesus before the members of the Sanhedrin and the Roman rulers bears the marks of a pre-planned plot to get him out of the way (Mk. 14:53–15:20). The trial violated most of the rules of the Sanhedrin procedure: capital charges could be tried only during the day; and since capital cases had to be reviewed on the day

150

following the trial, they could not take place on the day before the Sabbath or a festival. The Sanhedrin when assembled consisted of seventy (or seventy-one) Pharisees and Sadducees, yet the trial of Jesus appears to have taken place before only a few of its members. The Gospel of John disposes of any kind of trial before the Sanhedrin; it has Jesus appear only before the high priests, Annas and Caiaphas.

The Sanhedrin, set up several centuries before the time of Jesus to secure justice for the Jewish people, could prescribe capital punishment by stoning for Jews who had committed religious crimes such as blasphemy. Civil crimes, such as sedition, were turned over to the Roman government and were punishable by crucifixion.

The rapid procedure of the trial of Jesus indicates a plot among the Temple clique, some Sanhedrin leaders, and the Roman rulers. The Temple leaders fear Jesus' popularity among his fellow men; if he is not killed, their Temple system with its profits for them will suffer. The Roman rulers know of Jesus' popularity with his followers; unless he is dealt with rapidly, they fear an insurrection. Judas has told the Sanhedrin leaders that Jesus has accepted the title of Messiah ("king of the Jews"), and it is on this charge of sedition that he is condemned to death.

"Are you the king of the Jews?" they ask Jesus. "Thou hast said," he replies. He does not deny himself as Messiah. He thus becomes a victim of the Roman soldiers in the courtyard. They spit on him, hit him with sticks, put a purple cloth and a wreath on him, and cry with derision, "Hail, O king of the Jews!"

Jesus is too tired to bear the heavy crosspiece of the cross from the courtyard to the hill of crucifixion, and Simon, a Cyrenian farmer (Mk. 15:21), carries it for him. (Jesus' tiredness here may indicate why he dies on the cross within three hours.) He refuses an opiate of wine and myrrh to deaden the pain of crucifixion; he endures his sufferings to the end. Between two robbers Jesus is crucified; on his cross is the label, "The King of the Jews." What a commentary crucifixion of these three men portrays: So often we put to death our worst and our best persons, but on what different charges!

The Temple clique, the Sanhedrin leaders, the Roman rulers have quieted a revolution among several million people assembled at the Passover festival. However, within a few days there begins the greatest religious revolution in history. By A.D. 70 the Temple was destroyed; by A.D. 125 the Sanhedrin ceased to be; by A.D. 486 the Roman Empire had collapsed. . . .

> 'Tis truth alone is strong:
> Though her portion be the scaffold,
> And upon the throne be wrong,
> Yet that scaffold sways the future. . . .[1]

Jesus was nailed to the cross at nine in the morning; from noon until three in the afternoon darkness covered

---

[1] From "The Present Crisis" by James Russell Lowell.

the land. Was this darkness a physical happening in nature? Or was this darkness a symbol of tragedy, foretold
by the words of Amos, the prophet: "In that day, saith
the Lord, I will cause the sun to go down at noon, and
I will darken the earth in the clear day"?

The curtain which stands before the Holy of Holies
in the Temple is torn as Jesus dies on the cross. Does this
imply that through Jesus' redemptive act on the cross,
the curtain between man and God is rent so that the
glory of God shines in the face of Jesus Christ for all men
to see?

As Jesus dies on the cross (Mk. 15:33–41; Mt. 27:45–
56; Lk. 23:44–49; Jn. 25–28), seven expressions from his
lips are recorded in the gospels: (1) "Father, forgive them;
for they know not what they do." (2) "Truly, I say to
you, today you will be with me in Paradise." (3) To his
mother he said, "Behold your son." To his disciple he
said, "Behold your mother." (4) "My God, my God,
why hast thou forsaken me?" (5) "I thirst." (6) "It is
finished." (7) "Father, into thy hands I commit my
spirit." This last expression, quoted from Psalm 31, shows
us what Christ's triumph means. His victory is that of a
righteous person who, as he faces the uncertain adventure of death, can say

> With silent, lifting mind I've trod
> The high untrespassed sanctity of space,
> Put out my hand and touched the face of God.[2]

[2] From "Sunward I've Climbed" by John Magee.

153

That evening as Jesus' body was given to Joseph of Arimathæa to place in a sepulcher for burial, the crafty clique of the Temple, the Sanhedrin, and the Roman rulers were saying, "Well, we are finally rid of him!". . . But another answer was to ring down the centuries!

✤ 40 ✤

THERE IS ONLY ONE SORROW

LÉON BLOY, the French Christian, once said, "There is only one sorrow, not to be a saint." That is why we do not mourn today for the death of Jesus; rather we rejoice that he was such a saint—yet more than a saint.

The four gospels agree that Jesus died on Friday afternoon, the day of preparation for the Sabbath. Joseph of Arimathæa, a member of a petty court, buried Jesus in his tomb before sundown, thus fulfilling the Mosaic law that bodies be buried the day of death, outside the city walls of Jerusalem. The tomb is sealed and a Roman guard is placed by it, giving the gospel story security against the theories that Jesus' body was stolen from the tomb, or that the story of his resurrection was a fraud.

As we think of Jesus' death and burial in A.D. 30, we are also contemplating the meaning of death for you and me. We see Jesus' life lived so unselfishly within thirty years: as we think of Jesus in his tomb we are not sorrowing but rejoicing that his few years were spent so richly. As we meditate on the short span of years we shall live on this planet, the thought of Jesus' life and death drives us to do the worth-while things we want accomplished . . . to be more kind and helpful to the people we meet . . . to live this day as though it were the last and the best day of our existence. We want to live our lives as courageously and dynamically in the years ahead as Jesus lived his thirty short years. As we contemplate his death and ours, we are driven to live more deeply. The contemplation of his death—and ours—enriches life. Life holds but one major sorrow—not to be a saint.

As Jesus' followers, we see death as a part of our total experience; it is never isolated as something separate from life; it is synonymous with selfless living. Said Jesus, "Whosoever shall lose his life . . . shall save it." In his daily living the Christian learns how to die. Said the apostle Paul, "I die daily." There is within each person a bundle of selfish desires from which he must die before he can appreciate the experience of being "resurrected" to a higher kind of living. The Christian graduates from his selfish personality to the type of self who says, "Life is too much trouble unless one can live for something big." Proper thought of death causes one to die to pride, suspicion, resentment, fear, jealousy; it resurrects one to a life filled with unselfish love. He who learns how to "die daily" will find it natural to meet death with a faith which says:

O Love, that wilt not let me go,
I rest my weary soul on Thee;
I give Thee back the life I owe,
That in Thine ocean depths its flow
May richer, fuller be.[1]

There is little mourning over Jesus' death in the New Testament, though large attention is given to his death. The way in which Jesus died on the cross leaves a dynamic impression on his interpreters. Paul's gospel centers almost entirely about the crucifixion and the resurrection. The Gospel of Mark devotes one fifth of its space to Jesus' "last week" at Jerusalem. The Epistle to the Hebrews centers its interpretation on the sacrificial death of Jesus. For these interpreters, the way Christ died seemed to set a seal on the way Christ lived. He who said, "Whosoever shall lose his life shall save it," "Let him take up his cross and follow me," "Greater love has no man than this, that a man lay down his life for his friends," "Forgive seventy times seven," "Thy will be done," was sincere in what he said. For Jesus' last words and deeds on the cross exemplified that his thoughts at this tragic moment of death were the thoughts he had taught in the intensity of living. Jesus through his faith in God and his attitude toward man had shown redemptive love in its highest focus. Death has no barriers for one filled with such love.

Our thoughts today about Jesus' death are not mourn-

[1] George Matheson, "O Love, That Wilt Not Let Me Go."

156

ful, for we know his death will be answered by the resurrection. After men have done their worst to him, God will do his best—God is not one to be defeated. A Christian's thoughts about his own death ought to enrich his life. Like Jesus, we should see life as "lent to be spent," as an adventure in which we see a saint as "one in whom Christ is felt to live again". . . .

Each Lenten pilgrimage allows Jesus' followers to climb the steep ascent to Golgotha, where they view again "that strange man upon his cross." It is from this knoll, however, that they are able to see afresh beyond the horizon where dawns the Easter morn!

—